50 Quranic Comforts FOR MUMS

Nazmina Dhanji

SUN BEHIND THE CLOUD
PUBLICATIONS LTD

In the Name of Allah, the All-Compassionate, the All-Merciful.
Peace and Blessings on His beloved Messenger, Muhammad (pbuh),
and his blessed progeny.

Published by Sun Behind The Cloud Publications Ltd
PO Box 15889, Birmingham, B16 6NZ

This edition first published in 2019
© Copyright Nazmina Dhanji

ISBN (print): 978-1-908110-60-2
ISBN (ebook): 978-1-908110-61-9

A CIP catalogue record of this book is available
from the British Library.

www.sunbehindthecloud.com
info@sunbehindthecloud.com

For my heartbeats

MUHAMMAD JAWAD, RAHMA AND JANNAH

CONTENTS

INTRODUCTION

My eldest daughter woke up excitedly this morning, bounding out of bed without waiting for me to wake her a few times as per usual: of course – it was her birthday! She came downstairs humming Happy Birthday to herself, optimistically expecting to see a beautiful, furry, black and white cat waiting for her as her birthday present. For the last four years, the only thing she has consistently asked me for every birthday and every Eid is a cat. As much as I would have loved to get her one, I am allergic to them (thank God!). She knew deep down, of course, that I wouldn't have got her one and quickly resigned herself to the fact, eagerly opening her other presents and cards. Truth be told and allergy aside, I can just about parent three children with my sanity intact, let alone add a permanent furry addition to the family. I think that would actually push me over the edge. As much as I like the look and feel of their soft, lithe bodies, and as much as I acknowledge the positive effects that nurturing a living creature can have on children, the mere thought of cleaning up feline poop, and fur all over the upholstery, makes me shudder. Having had a negative and very queasy experience cleaning up poop from a previous chicken-rearing venture a few years ago, I swore I would clean up nothing more than my own children's mess henceforth.

Reminiscing over my little adventures in parenting children and chickens across different countries and the challenges that I have faced in my parenting journey are what actually led me to pen down some of those experiences, and share them with you. This book you hold in your hands can best be described as a collection of my musings and wonderings through this journey, written over several years, as a striving Muslim woman trying to parent my children in the 21st century, whilst maintaining the faith and growing towards God with kids in tow. As much as our parents and elders have been, and continue to be, a great source of support and guidance to us, as the next generation we often find ourselves in unchartered territory and treading water against the current when parenting in this century of high-speed technology and social media, where our own parents feel quite lost. I have stumbled and fallen many times on my journey, grazed my knees and had to learn the hard way more often than not. I have also had to 'wing it' more times than I would like to admit, but have ultimately found a lot of comfort, inspiration and solace in the Qur'an: our book of universal values which points to the best course of action. Its timeless wisdom and truths have guided me where even my own wise parents cannot.

This book is not 'another parenting book', and I do not profess to speak from a place of authority or expertise in parenting, or on any topic for that matter, nor do I claim to have all the answers. I am but a struggling parent myself, sharing the Qur'anic words of advice and reassurance that have been a profound source of guidance and comfort to me along my personal journey - mostly in hindsight - in the hope that they might bring you peace too. At the time of publication, I have three children aged 10, 14 and 16, and have been through my fair share of challenges whilst parenting them, as I am sure you have too with yours. Compared to parents of more children, older children, and those with grandchildren, however, I am but a novice!

These pages have not been designed to be read cover to cover. Rather, they have been written and tailored precisely for busy mothers - and fathers too if they so wish - who often have no time to read the paper or their Twitter feeds, let alone a whole book! It is for you to keep by your bedside to dip into for daily inspiration and support, offering a different perspective or just some food for thought when you need it most. I recommend you read no more than one chapter a day. It does not have to be read chronologically, as each chapter stands alone as its own topic, and is no more than two to four pages long. They each begin with a verse of the Qur'an, and end with a supplication related to the topic from the tradition of the Prophet (pbuh) and his beloved family, that I have also found helpful myself.

For the translation of Qur'anic verses I have mostly used Qarai's *Phrase-by-Phrase Translation of the Qur'an*.

Writing has been both a therapeutic and cathartic exercise for me, and I have dedicated space at the end of each chapter for you to journal your ideas and reflections too, should you wish to, guided by points to aid you in thinking further. Take your time with each chapter, think about it, then write down your thoughts and wishes for your children, composing your own supplications for them. Your wise words from your personal experiences may just end up being a great gift to them when they, in turn, become parents.

Whilst there are a few practical tips peppered throughout it wherever relevant, this book does not set out to be an instruction manual in parenting or give advice on specific topics. You know your child best, and the practical strategies that have worked for me may not work for you. There are already a myriad of tips and strategies out there for everything from nursing to potty-training and discipline on the Internet, on Pinterest, parenting books and blogs, many of which I resort to, time and again. There are also some excellent textbook-style Islamic parenting manuals available that I would highly recommend and which have helped me immensely, such as *Raising Children* by Tahera Kassamali, *A Mother's Prayer* by Arifa Hudda and *Principles of Upbringing Children* by Ibrahim Amini, to mention but a few. This work is a humble offering to help parents delve deeper into their relationship with God through Qur'anic reflections, to give them reassurance and tranquillity, and to refuel them along their parenting journey.

May the Almighty accept all our efforts, and overlook our shortcomings. All Praise is due to Him for His guidance, and we would not have been guided had He not guided us.

Nazmina Dhanji
March 2019

{ 3 }

1. FIRST COMES LOVE...

كَتَبَ رَبُّكُمْ عَلَى نَفْسِهِ الرَّحْمَةَ.

Your Lord ordained compassion upon Himself.

(Sūra al-Anʿām 6:54)

"I will always love you" - these are words that I, and I am sure, you too say to your children on a regular basis. "Nothing you ever do will make me stop loving you. I may be disappointed at your actions, but I will always love you," or other words to that effect.

Every single time I say this to my children, I am reminded of God's continuous and unending love for me in my own life, and that in spite of all my gaffes, stumbles, misdemeanours and outright sins, He has still not given up on me. Even when I did not obey at His first request, when I questioned His commands, He patiently and compassionately continued to love and nurture me, to guide me with His unconditional love, which overcame me.

What drew me to a conscious relationship with God in my late teens, and to surrender to His love, was not His rules but His own gracious invitation towards me, and the knowledge that in spite of my shortcomings and imperfections, He loved me and wanted only the best for me. "*He loves you seventy times more than your own mother*", we would be taught by our teachers, "*Just take one step towards Him, and He'll take ten back towards you.*" He says Himself that He has ordained love and *raḥma* (compassion) upon Himself. He is love. He is the very definition of compassion, being *Raḥmān* and *Raḥīm* (all-Compassionate and Merciful) - His primary attributes that we state at least 30 times each day. Accepting God's love for me was the impetus that then led to my wilful obedience of His commands and my desire to earn His pleasure.

This is precisely why our children need to be reminded of our unconditional love for them. They need first and foremost a relationship and an attachment to us, before we can give them a list of do's and don'ts. Our rules and discipline must be administered consequent to our love. Rigid rules may refine, and even change their behaviour, but they will not change the heart. Our children need us to pursue them patiently and lovingly, even when they don't deserve it, and most of all, when they have pushed us to the end of our tether and we're about to lose it with them.

What does that kind of unconditional love look like? Allah says: "*And He is with you wherever you are*" (Sūra al-Ḥadīd 57:4) - ready to listen to us. We too need to be willing to be there whenever our children need us - love slows down and listens. Reaching our children's hearts requires our attention. To build that kind of loving bond, we must listen to their fears, their dreams, their hurts, their concerns, their small playground victories. Love encourages and spurs children, without squashing them in the process; inspires, casting a vision for doing better through compassion.

God's love is what has motivated me to be obedient and come back to Him, each time that I have distanced myself through my mistakes. Instead of harsh discipline that breaks the spirit, He has gently guided me back with His reminders and signs punctuating my day. It fascinates me that although He speaks of His wrath, anger and disappointment in the Qur'an, above all He is *Raḥmān* and *Raḥīm* - just like a mother who scolds only out of her love, and only to the extent necessary. Let His gentle patience and compassionate corrections remind us to do the same for those that He has entrusted in our care.

يَا رَبِّي...وتتَحَبَّبُ إِلَيَّ فَأَتَبَغَّضُ إِلَيْكَ، وتَتَوَدَّدُ إِلَيَّ فَلَا أَقْبَلُ مِنْكَ
كَأَنَّ لِيَ التَطَوُّلَ عَلَيْكَ
فَلَمْ يَمْنَعْكَ ذَلِكَ مِنَ الرَّحْمَةِ لِي وَالإِحْسَانِ إِلَيَّ والتَّفَضُّلِ عَلَيَّ...
فَارْحَمْ عَبْدَكَ الْجَاهِلَ وَجُدْ عَلَيْهِ بِفَضْلِ إِحْسَانِكَ.

My Lord... You display Your love for me and I do not respond,
as though I am above You.
But this does not prevent You from having mercy on me, being good
to me, and favouring me... so please continue to be compassionate on
this ignorant slave of yours...

(Extract from Du'a al-Iftitah, usually recited in the month of Ramadan)

» How have you felt God's love for you in your life?

» Do you struggle to show that kind of 'unconditional' love
to your children?

» In what ways could you express that love to your children
right now?

2. TURNING WORRY INTO WORSHIP

وَأَصْبَحَ فُؤَادُ أُمِّ مُوسَى فَارِغًا إِنْ كَادَتْ لَتُبْدِيْ بِهِ لَوْلَا أَنْ رَبَطْنَا عَلَى قَلْبِهَا لِتَكُونَ مِنَ الْمُؤْمِنِيْن

And the heart of Musa's mother became empty (of anxiety); she would almost have disclosed it had We not reinforced her heart so that she would be of the believers.

(Sūra al-Qaṣaṣ 28:10)

I think I have the worry and anxiety gene, and I am sure I got it from my mother and my grandmother. They both passed down to me their youthful skin (thank God!), the dimple on their chins, and their tendency to worry.

When I was growing up, the Gujrati phrase '*mané evi viyadhi thaay tse*' (I am feeling so worried) was an almost daily phrase that could be heard in the house, and as a carefree teenager it never even occurred to me to question what worried my dear mother so much. But now as a mother, I find myself humming the same refrain, my mind wandering off into anxieties and fears about the unknown and uncontrollable future.

We mums can find endless reasons to worry: Kids. Marriage. Finances. Our kids' future careers. Our health. Theirs. The health of their faith. Even their future relationships! If we allow our thoughts to run wild, we can concoct all sorts of terrible scenarios, all starting with "What if?" *What if I lose my job? What if I miscarry? What if something's wrong with my baby's development? What if something happens to my parents tomorrow? What if he fails his subjects at school? What if she doesn't get in to the school of our choice?*

However, over time I have noticed something funny: 99 percent of my past fears never materialised, in spite of the oodles of time I spent fretting about them. How much time and energy I devoted to just sitting and ruminating.

Now contrast my attitude with Yukabad, the mother of Prophet Musa (pbuh), who had actual cause to worry as she threw her baby into the fast-flowing Nile in nothing but a little reed casket. A thousand thoughts could have been going through her mind at once: *"Am I doing the right thing? What if the basket capsizes? What if the water seeps into it and soaks him? What if the guards capture him? Will I ever see him again? What if he drowns? What about the hungry crocodiles?"*

The Qur'an tells us that her heart was empty. Perhaps she was so overcome with grief that she went blank, and froze in that moment, and that's why it's described as empty. It is far more likely, however, that *she* emptied it of worry and concern after Allah says above that He reinforced her heart (literally: bound it up). She emptied it, not out of a carelessness or nonchalance, but rather out of a confidence that God would return her baby to her, and that He would look after him. There was a lightness in her heart even despite the bleak and dangerous future ahead for both her and her baby. She trusted in God, and in His assurances that He never lets down the believers.

The one type of worry for our children that the Qur'an does warrant, however, is the worry for their faith. We see in the example of Prophet Ibrahim (pbuh), a father who mentions his children and future progeny at every opportunity in his supplications to Allah: 'O Allah, keep me and my children away from idolatry!' (Sūra Ibrahim 14:35) 'Make them upholders of the prayer!' (Sūra Ibrahim 14:40) And asking Him, 'Will they be leaders of the pious?' (Sūra al-Baqara 2:124) and making a bequest to his children, 'Don't you dare die except as submitters to God.' (Sura al-Baqara 2:132). When it came to the health and safety of their children's faith, even prophets worried. And they too turned their worry into worship.

So, what has been stealing your thoughts, keeping you up late at night and weighing heavy on your heart? What do you need to cast onto the God who rescued Prophet Musa from the clutch of a tyrant, Prophet Ibrahim from the blaze of a fire, Prophet Ayyub from infectious disease and bankruptcy, and Prophet Yunus from the corrosive belly of the whale? He loves the believer beyond comprehension and promises to rescue her from her worries in the same way that He rescued Prophet Yunus (pbuh): 'So We responded to him and saved him from distress, and thus do We save the believers' (Sūra al-Anbiyā' 21:88). He readily sustains and guides us as we voice our worries to Him.

God can use our tendency to worry to grow our faith. As we learn to turn our panic into fervent prayer and praise, our energy wasted on worry into concerted supplication and conversation with God, and trusting God's plan and His timing, we find that our relationship with God is strengthened. Each time we turn worry into worship, we will find it easier to handle our anxieties and wilfully empty our hearts of worries. Our act of trust in Him, especially with our precious children and their futures, is a true manifestation of professing faith in God. He knows each and every fibre of our being. Every moment that we clutch tightly in desperate fear to control, He already has it under control. Let go my friend, He's got this.

رَبَّنَا عَلَيْكَ تَوَكَّلْنَا وَإِلَيْكَ أَنَبْنَا وَإِلَيْكَ الْمَصِيرُ

Our Lord, in You we place our trust, to You we turn,
and towards You is the destination.

(Sūra al-Mumtaḥana 60:4)

⋙⌐ What are your three greatest worries as a parent? List them

⋙⌐ Take each of these worries, and pen a prayer to God instead.
Note how your heart feels when you do this.

3. THE JONESES ARE OVERRATED

وَلَا تَمُدَّنَّ عَيْنَيْكَ إِلَى مَا مَتَّعْنَا بِهِ أَزْوَاجًا مِنْهُمْ زَهْرَةَ الْحَيَاةِ الدُّنْيَا لِنَفْتِنَهُمْ فِيهِ، وَرِزْقُ رَبِّكَ خَيْرٌ وَأَبْقَى

And do not stretch your gaze to that which We have provided certain groups to enjoy as the glitter of the life of this world, so that We may test them thereby. And the provision of Your Lord is better and more lasting.

(Sūra Ṭāhā: 131)

As I caught up on my Facebook feed while waiting to pick up the kids from school, a friend had posted: 'Seared teriyaki wagyu beef, with a side of garlic-tossed green beans from the garden, and my famous key-lime pie to finish it off - another dinner party success!' Another posed in front of the Ka'ba in photos of a family trip to Umra - one of many, while another gushed: 'Yay! My son's been awarded student of the month!'

Incidentally, I was going through a particularly rough time that month - struggling to pay bills after unforeseen costs, barely having time to pop a pizza and fish fingers in the oven, desperately craving a break that couldn't be remedied by a Kit-Kat, or a weekend away even to Bognor Regis, and getting regular phone calls home from my son's school about his flagrant disregard for school uniform rules. At that moment, my life sucked, compared to the Facebook Joneses and their friends!

In our parents' days, we only saw the Joneses a few times a week. Maybe we would bump into them in the car park at the mosque as we parked our Datsun Cherry next to their new Mercedes, or perhaps at a mutual friend's wedding. Now they parade in front of our eyes nearly twenty-four hours a day on our news feeds and smartphones; on Twitter, Facebook, Pinterest and Instagram. The Joneses used to be more discrete with their acquisitions, awards and holidays, but now their 'Look at me!' snaps are splashed all over our screens and their profile-picture-perfect lives can tempt us to feel disdain and discontent that would never otherwise cross our minds. Yes, the Joneses definitely invade our homes and our thoughts several times a day through social media and rob us of our peace of mind.

God, however, already warned us about the Joneses in the above verse, which I have to keep reminding myself about every time I feel like this. And every time I read it, I am taken aback at how God's commandment to avert our eyes does not apply only to those things that are explicitly forbidden, but also to things that may upset our inner peace, that may cause us turmoil, take away our contentment, and disturb us. I remember being advised by someone to be especially careful about what I looked at whilst pregnant, avoiding disturbing scenes of war, crime, accidents and even festering rubbish heaps!

That is understandable as those kind of things are actually and immediately disturbing. Images of the Joneses exotic holidays and all that God has '*provided certain groups to enjoy as the glitter of the life of this world*' seem harmless when casually scrolling through Instagram. But those images can linger on the mind, causing lurking envy towards others who have done nothing wrong, and potentially, discontentment with our own blessings. He knows fully how we operate as humans, and that we make comparisons by our very nature. Have you noticed how our children compare new shoes, bicycles, how high they can jump, how fast they can run, their biceps and how many friends they have?

Even as adults, comparisons come quite easily within our own fields. Doctors compare themselves not against electricians and lawyers but against other doctors. The same goes for bloggers and pastry chefs, and parents are no exception. We live in an increasingly competitive culture, so comparisons come easily and seem to be encouraged. We compare our parenting, our kids, our homes, the books we read, our spiritual journeys and a whole host of other things. Hence Allah advises us with His truth and wisdom: *Do not stretch your eyes…* - especially when you've had a hard day and especially when you're already feeling low. Peeking into the lives of others to see how we are measuring up never helps. So, what can we do instead on days like that?

He gave us an answer to that too: focus on *'the provision'* that He has already given us. Focus on Him. When we take our eyes off other people's plates, we can focus them better on our own. True, our plates may look sparse and miserable at this moment in time, but it is only then that we will be humble enough to ask: 'Why have You put this on my plate? What are You trying to teach me?' Or even look to someone else's even emptier plate, and say: 'Thank you, Lord!' or even, 'How can I help?'

We can only do this when we stop stretching our eyes to the Joneses and turn our eyes to God, and His provision.

رَبِّ أَوْزِعْنِي أَنْ أَشْكُرَ نِعْمَتَكَ الَّتِي أَنْعَمْتَ عَلَيَّ وَعَلَىٰ وَالِدَيَّ وَأَنْ أَعْمَلَ صَالِحًا تَرْضَاهُ

وَأَدْخِلْنِي بِرَحْمَتِكَ فِي عِبَادِكَ الصَّالِحِينَ.

My Lord! Inspire me to give thanks for Your blessing with which You have blessed me and my parents,
and that I may do righteous deeds which please You,
And admit me, by Your mercy, among Your righteous servants.

(Sūra al-Naml 27:19)

>>> Have you ever felt discontentment with what's on your plate when reading others' posts on social media?

>>> How have you dealt with it in the past?

>>> How will asking: "Lord, what are you trying to teach me?" help you battle discontentment?

4. WHAT MAKES A HOME?

وَاللَّـهُ جَعَلَ لَكُم مِّن بُيُوتِكُمْ سَكَنًا...

It is Allah who has made your homes a place of rest for you...

(Sūra al-Naḥl 16:80)

Whenever I pick up my children from their grandparents' houses after they've been babysitting, I enter expecting to see the same war zone that my own home witnesses at times, but instead am greeted with, 'They're as good as gold when you're not here', 'They were absolutely fine'. Maybe that has something to do with the endless supply of snacks, TV shows and grandparents' mellow magic, but I've been hearing the same from when they were babies. 'She was fine! Kids only play up in their own homes'.

Now there's an element of truth here, that all of us feel most at ease and comfort in our own homes, especially children, free to let out screams and stifled burps, and express anguishes, and whatever else has been bothering them deep down; and so it seems that they save it all for when they get home. The minute we enter the house, suddenly everything hurts them, and there are complaints and whinges from every side. As noisy and messy as a home is, there is something comfortable and 'homely' about home that simply cannot be replicated elsewhere. What is it then that makes a house a home, I wondered?

I posed the question to my teens, only having moved into our current house about a year ago: 'What is it that has made this new house a home?' My son dramatically remarked that he had lived in eight different houses by the time he had turned fourteen, and for a place to feel like home, one had to have lived in it for at least a couple of years, so he was essentially 'home'less! Although not entirely true, he was right in the fact that we had moved so often, they had never lived in one house for more than a couple of years. So does length of time factor into what makes a house a home? Or is it rather about the memories that we have made in those places? My daughter piped up that she did not even remember some of the houses we had lived in, and had no memories of those 'homes' besides the odd photo here and there. 'Home is where the heart is', said my daughter – clearly the result of a clichéd google search result. 'Home is wherever you hang your hat', piped up my son, cheekily.

After going back and forth for a few minutes, we concluded that although our addresses – some of them across continents -, décor, furniture, walls and carpets had changed and had no sense of permanence to them, there were certain constants in each place we had inhabited that had made them homes. Sure, we had not 'set down roots' in any one physical place yet, but the roots of faith and tranquillity in our home had taken priority over those. We agreed that a strong sense of rootedness in a home came from our values, and our sense of security and safety in it as the place where we felt most love and acceptance.

It is important for children to see and feel their home as a safe place where they can be fully themselves. Besides basic needs of food, water and shelter, human beings also have essential emotional needs that must be fulfilled: security, belonging and a sense of purpose. Food, drink and shelter can be had elsewhere, but home is where these emotional needs are fully met, where they are loved and cared for despite the storms raging outside. Home is where they can talk about their fears, doubts and all the things that threaten their peace, where they can safely release pent-up stress, and even guffaws of laughter. Home, in the safety of their parents' guidance and care, is a place where no subject is too taboo: bullying, injustices, drugs, homelessness, racism, sex, prejudice, alcohol, crime, vices, and so on, can all be discussed with ease. Home is where parents offer children security and shelter; *'a place of rest for you'* as Allah calls it – from the word *sukoon* (tranquillity), chaotic and messy as it may look on the surface. And if the home does not provide a safe space to be who they are and be loved unconditionally, then they will either look for that elsewhere or numb its absence.

As we adorn our houses with plush carpets, eye-friendly colour palettes, and feature walls, considering where to hang the art and the photos of our children to make it as 'homely' as possible, let us remember the other ingredients that make a house into a home.

رَبِّ ابْنِ لِيْ عِنْدَكَ بَيْتًا فِي الْجَنَّةِ

My Lord, build for me with You a home in Paradise

(Sūra al-Taḥrīm 66:11 - Lady Asiya's beautiful supplication for a home with God in Paradise, despite living in palaces in the world)

> **What special ingredient do you feel makes your house a home?**

> **What can you start - or stop - doing today to bring more peace into your home?**

5. GOD'S MOTIVATIONAL SPEECH
(بُشْرَى)

وَلَنَبْلُوَنَّكُمْ بِشَيْءٍ مِنَ الْخَوْفِ وَالْجُوعِ وَنَقْصٍ مِنَ الأَمْوَالِ وَالأَنْفُسِ وَالثَّمَرَاتِ وَبَشِّرِ الصَّابِرِينَ.

And We will most certainly test you with a measure of fear and hunger, and loss of property, lives and fruit; and give good news to the patient.

(Sūra al-Baqara 2:155)

There is no doubt that there are parts of parenthood that feel so taxing at times that it takes all our effort to 'suffer through' them, and this test seems to be a universal one that even the greatest of God's prophets had to undergo, such as Prophet Nuh and Prophet Ya'qub. As taxing and wearisome as the physical strain of nursing a sick child is, or the mental strain of shrill cries, constant whinging and endless worry, or the emotional turmoil of a rebellious child who tests every last nerve, or any of the challenges that we as humans will necessarily have to undergo, we have to remind ourselves that in this 'suffering' lies tremendous growth. The unattractive parts of life hold opportunities for us to hear Allah's *bushrā*, often translated as 'glad tidings' or 'good news', or which I prefer to translate as 'His motivational speech'. Sometimes due to the din in our heads, we are unable to hear that soothing voice inside encouraging us to persevere, consoling us to take heart and that He will reward us for our pains, motivating us to persevere as He does in the verse above. He reserves that special *bushrā* for the patient ones who persevere through their challenges.

So when will these rewards or glad tidings come? What does that *bushrā* and divine motivation look like? His rewards are not dependent on other people noticing our efforts and commending us for them - He Himself notes the act of service, of perseverance, of working hard in that very moment and blesses us in that very moment as we vacuum, clean up after our children, juggle difficult situations - we are blessed right in the midst of it all by way of spiritual growth. He recognises and sees what no one else does, and rewards abundantly in ways unimaginable, for He himself accompanies us in that moment: 'Indeed God is **with** the patient ones' (Sūra al-Baqara 2:153), He says, and 'Indeed **with** difficulty is ease' (Sūra al-Inshirāḥ 94:5-6). He reassures Prophets Musa and Haroon (pbut) in the midst of facing a tyrannical bully, 'I am with you: I hear and see' (Sūra Ṭā Hā 20:46). Perhaps we need to attune ourselves to the notion that the rewards we anticipate as piles of gold coins or brownie points that will allow us entrance into Paradise somewhere in the distant future is happening right here and now in the thick of our challenges; just like the beautiful calm in the eye of the storm. He is *al-Laṭīf* (The Gentle One) and *al-Khafiyy* (The Discreet One), and He softly and discreetly dispels worries and calms the heart, even when it seems you'll never surmount this.

Just as we parents have a wide inventory of tools to motivate our reluctant children to action, from sticker charts and treats, to threats of punishment and removal of privileges, so does Allah cater for all His creatures, with all their varying levels of moral development. To some He promises rewards, others He motivates through stories and parables, and yet others through logical explanations. Some need only gentle reminders of His proximity and pleasure, whilst the harder nuts among us require threats of punishment. And even then, like a kind parent would do, He gently adds in a disclaimer and nudges them to correct action: 'Why should Allah chastise you if you are grateful and believe?' (Sūra al-Nisā' 4:147). Why would He punish you when He's the one rooting for you, pushing you to grow, just like we do not intervene and pick up our children at every stumble and fall, every cry and wail, so that they may discover their strengths, develop tolerance and grit, and learn from their mistakes.

Even the suffering that we encounter in life through bereavement, persecution, strife, tragedy and pain are not losses but valuable training as we are moulded into the very best versions of our selves. And through it all, He continues to speak to us and to motivate us: 'Don't be sad. Surely, God is with us!' (Sūra al-Tawba 9:40). Let us mute the frustration, press pause, and tune our ears to His *bushrā*.

الَّذِينَ إِذَا أَصَابَتْهُمْ مُصِيبَةٌ قَالُوا إِنَّا لِلهِ وَإِنَّا إِلَيْهِ رَاجِعُوْنَ

Those who, when a misfortune befalls them, say: Surely we are Allah's and to Him we are surely returning.

(Sūra al-Baqara 2:156)

(This is the continuation of the verse above, where Allah describes the patient ones' mantra when they face difficulty - they remind themselves that they are His, and are always in the process of returning to Him.
This is how they motivate themselves.)

᠁ How can you approach your tasks and care for your children differently now that you know this?

᠁ What are some of your favourite āyāt or quotes that you use to motivate you?

6. CONFLICTING PARENTING STYLES

قُلْ يَا أَهْلَ الْكِتَابِ تَعَالَوْا إِلَى كَلِمَةٍ سَوَاءٍ بَيْنَنَا وَبَيْنَكُمْ أَلَّا نَعْبُدَ إِلَّا

اللهَ وَلَا نُشْرِكَ بِهِ شَيْئًا وَلَا يَتَّخِذَ بَعْضُنَا بَعْضًا أَرْبَابًا مِنْ دُوْنِ اللهِ...

Say: O People of the Book, come to a common ground between us and
you: that we shall not worship any but Allah, and that we shall not
associate aught with Him, and that some of us will not take others as
lords besides Allah...

(Sūra Āl ʿImrān 3:64)

There are as many ways to parent as there are personalities out
there, and as many opinions on the 'best way to parent' as there are
parents! Even the most easy-going of parents, however, are bound to
have differences of opinion with their other halves when it comes to
choosing what is best for their beloved offspring, who are equal parts
of both. A mother may feel that as she spends the most time with
them, they grew inside of her, she feels that she knows her children
best to their very core, and hence what is 'best for them', whereas their
father has equal right to what he feels is best for them given his unique
perspective.

It is inevitable for parenting styles between spouses to differ, as we
often parent the way we were parented, or sometimes diametrically
opposite to the way we were parented. Our decisions as parents
may also be motivated by our own desires: to have our children be
a source of pride for us, to reflect the good job we did raising them,
to realise some of our own dreams through them. They may equally
be motivated by our fears for the future and to protect them from
potential dangers that our generations never faced. If there are two or
more children in the household, chances are you will have to parent

each child differently based on their own individual personality. Our parenting may also be influenced by significant people in their lives: grandparents, the in-laws, other caregivers and even your own peers.

Sometimes making important decisions can be overwhelming when the combination of all these different factors have the potential to cause strife when it comes to choosing the right school, or the right way to discipline, or whether to give pocket money or not, whether to allow sleepovers or not, how to handle meltdowns and tantrums, how much screen time to allow. The last thing a couple needs, however, is disagreement and strife, especially in front of the children.

Being on the same page as our spouses, even if we have conflicting ideas about parenting or we have had very different upbringings, is crucial. To contradict each other in front of the children, or to argue about these things in the midst of important parenting decisions can be no less shambolic than Brexit negotiations, and children can and do play parents off against one another. With our own desires and fears thrown into the mix, along with other people's opinions and 'expert' views, it is very easy to lose sight of the fact that you both ultimately want what's best for your children and the bigger picture becomes blurred.

Our Prophet (pbuh) modelled this for us very diplomatically in his dealings and debates with people of different creeds and religions, where there was far more at stake. As highlighted in the verse above, he resolved these conflicts with open conversation and communication, inviting people to talk about it and to find common ground without having to compromise his values. He advocated for a back-to-basics approach of starting off with shared beliefs and values, and building up from there with the utmost humility and grace. Like him, we too can look at the bigger picture by focusing on the commonalities, the values that both parents hold dear, and their ultimate common goal of raising God-conscious children, then agree on the policies from that base.

رَبَّنَا آتِنَا مِنْ لَّدُنْكَ رَحْمَةً وَّهَيِّئْ لَنَا مِنْ أَمْرِنَا رَشَدًا.

Our Lord! Grant us mercy from You and provide for us a right course in our decision

(The supplication for guidance made by the Companions of the Cave when they were faced with a difficult decision - Sūra al-Kahf 18:10)

- Whilst you both want 'the best' for your kids, what common values do you and your spouse both agree on?

- What do you both ultimately want for your children?

- Where can you identify potential areas of conflict between you when it comes to the kids, and where could you meet in the middle?

7. WE HAVE TO OR WE GET TO?

مَنْ عَمِلَ صَالِحًا مِنْ ذَكَرٍ أَوْ أُنْثَى وَهُوَ مُؤْمِنٌ فَلَنُحْيِيَنَّهُ حَيَوةً طَيِّبَةً وَلَنَجْزِيَنَّهُمْ أَجْرَهُمْ بِأَحْسَنِ مَا كَانُوْا يَعْمَلُوْنَ.

Whoever does good, whether male or female, being a believer, We will most certainly make him live a happy life, and We will most certainly give them their reward for the best of what they used to do.

(Sūra al-Naḥl 16:97)

My roles as a wife, daughter, mother, sister, teacher, translator, taxi driver, neighbour and friend bring me much joy, but they also bring with them lots of to-do lists. Meals to cook, purchases to make, meetings to organise, lessons to plan, research to undertake, kids to taxi around, phone calls to make, bills to pay, and on and on the lists grow. And as they get longer on the paper I scribble them on, the self-pitying martyr inside me rears her exasperated head and starts looping the 'poor me' soundtrack on repeat.

Poor me... I have so much paperwork to finish.

Poor me... I have so much homework to mark.

Poor me... I have to drive the kids to gymnastics and maths tuition.

Poor me... I have to cook for guests.

Poor me... I have so much laundry to fold and iron.

Poor, poor, pitiful me!

God reminds us of some important truths about our actions in the verse above as well as in many other similar verses, and indirectly addresses this 'poor me' mentality by giving us a fresh perspective as we go about our daily work. He tells us that no one's hard work is wasted (Sūra Āl 'Imrān 3:95; Sūra al-Kahf 18:30), that He watches our deeds and recompenses every little thing done for Him; that we ourselves will witness every atom's worth of good that we do (Sūra al-Zilzāl 99:7-8). He reminds us that whatever good we do is ultimately for our own souls, (Sūra Fussilat 41:46; Sūra al-Jāthiya 45:15), - not just the tasks we enjoy, or the work that brings credit and recognition, or the duties that we happen to find fun, but *whatever* we do that is good and productive, even if we do not yet see the fruits of our labours.

How about we hit the stop button on our looping 'poor me' track, and press the play button on our tasks instead? We can choose not to see ourselves as martyrs but to instead reframe our attitudes:

I don't *have* to clean my house. I *get* to clean my house - because I have a place to call my own, while many are homeless or displaced. And I'm serving my family for the sake of God while I clean.

I don't *have* to drive my kids to gymnastics. I *get* to do so, because my children are healthy enough for physical activity and we are blessed to have a car.

I don't *have* to cook for guests. I *get* to have guests over, because God blessed us with friends and family, and surplus to share with others.

Instead of seeing our work, tasks and even the unpleasant chores as things we *have* to do, let us embrace our roles and be grateful for the fact that He has blessed us with the opportunity to *get* to do them in the first place, on top of which He promises us a good life and a reward!

اللّهُمَّ صَلِّ عَلَى مُحَمَّدٍ وَّآلِه وَاكْفِنِيْ مَا يَشْغَلُنِيْ الْاِهْتِمَامُ بِه وَاسْتَعْمِلْنِيْ بِمَا تسْأَلُنِيْ غَدًا عَنْهُ، وَاسْتَفْرِغْ أَيَّامِيْ فِيْمَا خَلَقْتَنِيْ لَهُ، وَأَغْنِنِيْ وَأَوْسِعْ عَلَيَّ فِيْ رِزْقِكَ...

O God, bless Muhammad and His household, and spare me the concerns that distract me, employ me in that which You will ask me about tomorrow, and let me pass my days for that which You have created me. Free me from need and expand Your provision toward me.

(Extract from Imam Zayn al-Abidin (pbuh)'s Supplication for Noble Moral Traits Du'a Makārim al-Akhlāq)

ᴡᴡᴦ **Name one 'have to' item that is on your to-do list today. How could you turn your thoughts about this task into a thankful 'I get to' statement instead?**

_____

_____

_____

_____

_____

_____

8. PROUD PARENTS AND SERVANTS

سَلَامٌ عَلَى إِبْرَاهِيْمَ. كَذَلِكَ نَجْزِيْ الْمُحْسِنِيْنَ.
إِنَّهُ مِنْ عِبَادِنَا الْمُؤْمِنِيْنَ.

Peace be upon Ibrahim. Thus do we reward the doers of good.
Indeed he was one of Our believing servants.

(Sūra al-Ṣāffāt 37:109-111)

As my son stood tall in a firefighter's uniform, certificate in hand after having completed a life-skills training course in a fire station over the past week, towering above me and bending down to give me a hug, the past fifteen years of his seemed to flash before my eyes. My heart swelled with pride as I reminisced over the day that this handsome young man was born: the day that witnessed my own birth into motherhood. The joys, the tears, the many, many sleepless nights, the intensity of our bond, and even the many arguments that came along the way, flashed before my eyes, and I whispered, 'I am so proud of you'. I spent the rest of that day gushing about his achievement and award, sending pictures of him holding his certificate to the extended family as he lapped up all the congratulations and love that came his way. Needless to say, his grandparents' hearts swelled with even more pride than my own!

Although it is so natural to feel proud of our children's achievements, Prophet Ibrahim (pbuh)'s story in the Qur'an opened my eyes to a deeper dimension to the pride that I was feeling. He is one prophet in the Qur'an that God talks about ever so proudly. God does not merely recount the stories of His prophets in the Qur'an in a factual, chronological way, but rather gushes proudly, praises them, and blesses them, such as when He mentions Prophet Ayyub, He exclaims: 'How wonderful the servant is! Frequently he turned to Us' (Sūra Ṣād 38:44), or 'Peace be upon Ibrahim' (Sūra al-Ṣāffāt 37:109). Then He proceeds to tell us *why* He's so proud of them: 'Indeed he is one of Our believing servants' (Sūra al-Ṣāffāt 37:111). God even quotes Prophet Ibrahim's words verbatim, detailing exactly how he stood up to the idol-worshippers who bullied him and what he said to them (Sūra al-Shu'arā 26:78-82). You can literally hear God's pride coming across and He makes it known to us exactly *what* He was proud of him for.

As clued-up parents in the modern day, despite being conscious of loving our children unconditionally, independently of good grades, achievements, medals, trophies, sporting wins, etc. in the midst of our parental pride, it is very easy to showcase the physical manifestations of their achievements whilst leaving the *why* in the locker room. Allah teaches us how important it is to mention the *why*, how to commend our children for the qualities that they demonstrate rather than the outcome. My son's trainer made it a point to commend his stamina, his willingness to help his teammates, his taking initiative and his bravery, and although those were the very reasons for my own maternal pride inside, I'm not sure that came across to him when his photo of him with certificate and medal in hand took centre-stage that day. In hindsight, it would have been even better to let him 'overhear' me telling my family members what his trainer said about him, so that he knew without a shadow of doubt that his mother's pride lay not in the medals and trophies, but in the noble qualities and hard work that he had displayed. It is ever so important to praise our children for their continuous efforts over and above just the achievements that we are proud of.

It is not just His prophets that God is proud of. He is proud of us too, and actually boasts to His angels about His sincere servants, for the very same reasons: the patience, perseverance, resilience, sincerity, kindness and steadfastness that they display. God's pride is values-based and effort-based, and so must ours be, both in our pride for our children, but also ourselves.

كَفَى بِيْ عِزًّا أَنْ أَكُوْنَ لَكَ عَبْدًا وَكَفَى بِيْ فَخْرًا أَنْ تَكُوْنَ لِيْ رَبًّا. إِلهِيْ
أَنْتَ كَمَا أُحِبُّ فَاجْعَلْنِيْ كَمَا تُحِبُّ.

*It is enough of an honour for me to be Your servant, and it is enough
pride for me that You are my Lord. My God, You are exactly as I love,
so make me as You would love me to be.*

(Supplication by Imam Ali (pbuh) recommended to recite in the last *sajda* of *salat*
where we express our pride at being His servants and ask Him to mould us into
servants that He can be proud of)

- **Are you proud to be God's servant? Do you feel proud of what you have been tasked with?**

- **Can you think of ways in which you could extract the qualities and efforts that your child displayed in their most recent achievement?**

- **How could you express them to your child in creative ways?**

9. A WORK OF ART

خَلَقَ السَّمَاوَاتِ وَالْأَرْضَ بِالْحَقِّ ۚ وَصَوَّرَكُمْ فَأَحْسَنَ صُوَرَكُمْ ۖ
وَإِلَيْهِ الْمَصِيرُ.

He is the One who created the heavens and the earth with the truth.
And He fashioned you all and designed you in the best form.
And to Him is the final destination.

(Sūra al-Taghābun 64:3)

I came across a poem the other day that one of my daughters had composed for me on Mothers' Day a few years ago. She had taken the time to write it in a Jamaican reggae style that had to be rapped, carefully selecting the words to make it rhyme, writing, editing and revising it over several days. She had even gotten over her shyness and rapped it for me! It was called: *Wha Me Mudda Do* (all about the things that I do for her). I loved that poem so much because it was my daughter's handiwork, a product of her thought and a reminder of the love that she expressed to me that day; just as I have loved all the cards, poems, messages and breakfasts-in-bed that my children have designed and made for me over the years.

Now I am not a very sentimental person when it comes to keeping birthday cards, and there are very few objects of purely sentimental value that I will keep for a long time, but the handmade cards and poems that my children have made me over the years I cherish and have a whole drawer dedicated to keeping them forever. There is something magical in the action of imagining, creating, designing and making something original from scratch, and in that God-given ability, we manifest His divine qualities. He is 'The Master-Designer' (*al-Muṣawwir*), 'the Creator' (*al-Khāliq*) and 'The Originator' (*al-Fāṭir*). In the verse above and in many such verses, God states that just as He created the vast heavens and the earth and all the beauty and majesty that they contain, so has He designed and fashioned us in the best of forms. We are His work of art, His design, His *chef-d'oeuvres*.

God, however, did not design and create us as a one-time action to be filed away in a drawer like our children's artwork, but He continuously creates, designs and fashions. In the Hands of the Master-sculptor we have to be flexible and allow ourselves to be moulded, fashioned, stretched, and redefined as we trust that He creates us in the *best* form, and wants His masterpieces to be their best possible versions. God's act of creation is fluid and continuous, and when I remind myself of that, it allows me to be accepting of change, accepting of trials and challenges in my life. When I see myself as a unique work of art in progress, an individual bespoke masterpiece into which His divine plan and design is being infused, right from when I was in my mother's womb, it makes it easier to bear the sharpness of His pencil and to trust His swift brush strokes.

It also makes me more patient with my children's development. Often as parents, in all our expectations of wanting our children to be the best versions of themselves and hit milestones, we expect them to 'turn out' a certain way magically, overnight, forgetting that their development and coming into being takes time. God takes his time to fashion a great oak tree, a baby so tiny and even a bumblebee. He grows them ever so slowly so that we can see, and know the way we are to be. We are beautiful pieces of art in the Hands of the Master Artist. The plans He has prepared for you and I, and our children, are not yet finished!

فَأَيُّ نِعَمِكَ يَا اِلـٰهِى أُحْصى عَدَداً وَذِكْراً، أَمْ اَيُّ عَطاياكَ أَقُومُ بِها شُكْراً، وَهِيَ يَا رَبِّ اَكْثَرُ مِنْ اَنْ يُحْصِيَها الْعَادّونَ، أَوْ يَبْلُغَ عِلْماً بِها الْحافِظُونَ، ثُمَّ ما صَرَفْتَ وَدَرَأْتَ عَنِّى اَللّـٰهُمَّ مِنَ الضُّرِّ وَالضَّرّاءِ، أَكْثَرُ مِمّا ظَهَرَ لى مِنَ الْعافِيَةِ وَالسَّرّاءِ، وَاَنَا اَشْهَدُ يَا اِلـٰهِى بِحَقيقَةِ ايمانى، وَعَقْدِ عَزَماتِ يَقينى، وَخالِصِ صَريحِ تَوْحيدى، وَباطِنِ مَكْنُونِ ضَميرى، وَعَلائِقِ مَجارى نُورِ بَصَرى، وَاَسارِيرِ صَفْحَةِ جَبينى، وَخُرْقِ مَسارِبِ نَفْسى، وَخَذاريفِ مارِنِ عِرْنينى، وَمَسارِبِ سِماخِ سَمْعى، وَما ضُمَّتْ وَاَطْبَقَتْ عَلَيْهِ شَفَتاىَ، وَحَرَكاتِ لَفْظِ لِسانى، وَمَغْرَزِ حَنَكِ فَمى وَفَكّى، وَمَنابِتِ اَضْراسى، وَمَساغِ مَطْعَمى وَمَشْرَبى، وَحِمالَةِ اُمِّ رَأْسى، وَبُلُوغِ فارِغِ حَبائِلِ عُنُقى، وَمَا اشْتَمَلَ عَلَيْهِ تامُورُ صَدْرى، وَحمائِلِ حَبْلِ وَتينى، وَنِياطِ حِجابِ قَلْبى، وَاَفْلاذِ حَواشى كَبِدى، وَما حَوَتْهُ شَراسيفُ اَضْلاعى، وَحِقاقُ مَفاصِلى، وَقَبْضُ عَوامِلى، وَاَطْرافُ اَنامِلى وَلَحْمى وَدَمى، وَشَعْرى وَبَشَرى، وَعَصَبى وَقَصَبى، وَعِظامى وَمُخّى وَعُرُوقى، وَجَميعُ جَوارِحى، وَمَا انْتَسَجَ عَلى ذلِكَ اَيّامَ رَضاعى، وَما اَقَلَّتِ الْاَرْضُ مِنّى، وَنَوْمى وَيَقَظَتى وَسُكُونى وَحَرَكاتِ رُكُوعى وَسُجُودى، اَنْ لَوْ حاوَلْتُ وَاجْتَهَدْتُ مَدَى الْاَعْصارِ وَالْاَحْقابِ لَوْ عُمِّرْتُها اَنْ اُؤَدِّىَ شُكْرَ واحِدَة مِنْ اَنْعُمِكَ مَا اسْتَطَعْتُ ذلِكَ اِلّا بِمَنِّكَ الْمُوجَبِ عَلَىَّ بِهِ شُكْرُكَ اَبَداً جَديداً

Which of Your favours, O my God, can I count in numbers and examples? Or which of Your gifts can I thank properly?... from the lines of my forehead, the hallows of the courses of my breath, the cavities of my nose..., the motions of the vocalisation of my tongue, the socket of the palate of my mouth and jaw, the matrices of my teeth, the tasting of my food and my drink, ... the tube of the tissues of my neck, ...the carriers of the cord of my aorta, that which the cartilages of my ribs contains, the cavities of my joints, the seamless integration of my organs to the tip of my fingers, my flesh and blood, my hair and skin, my nerves and sinews, my bones and brain and veins, and all of my organs... my sleeping and wakefulness; (by all that I bear witness) that if I try my best and strive throughout all ages and all times, to thank properly only one of Your favours, I would not be able to.

(Extract from Duʾa ʿArafa by Imam Ḥusayn (pbuh) -
literally a poem detailing *Wha me God do!*)

⤛⤏ **In what ways do you think God is shaping you to bring out the beauty in you?**

⤛⤏ **Do you struggle to believe you are really God's 'handiwork'? If so, why do you think that is?**

10. NOT EVEN WATER?

يَا أَيُّهَا الَّذِينَ آمَنُوا كُتِبَ عَلَيْكُمُ الصِّيَامُ كَمَا كُتِبَ عَلَى الَّذِينَ مِنْ قَبْلِكُمْ لَعَلَّكُمْ تَتَّقُونَ.

O you who believe! Fasting has been prescribed for you as it was prescribed for those before you, so that you may be God-conscious.

(Sūra al-Baqara 2:183)

It's that time of year again when we have to explain to our non-Muslim friends and our children's teachers that yes, they are capable of fasting from around puberty; and yes, they understand what they are doing; and no, they are not being forced into it; and no, not even water.

Some parents have a relatively easy time teaching their *baligh* (mature) children to fast, where children willingly follow their example, without the need for elaborate bribes and distractions. My own children's resilience, wilful participation and perseverance has often pleasantly surprised me, though it is not something that I ever take for granted, as the same children have found it difficult the following year, and have needed more encouragement and reminders.

Other parents may persistently have a hard time motivating their children to fast, and having answers to the *but why*'s, even more so than having to explain to non-Muslims. This is all part of the process, and the main thing to remember is that fasting is supposed to be hard. It's not designed to be easy. It's supposed to present a challenge for us, so first and foremost, give yourself a firm pat on the back for fasting whilst looking after young children, having to wake everyone up for *suhoor* (the pre-dawn meal), dealing with extra grumpiness, having to shop and cook more, and generally having to be upbeat and excited despite your own lack of energy. You are doing a great job!

The internet is replete with ideas of how to make Ramadan exciting and meaningful for children, along with a multitude of tips on how to introduce fasting to little ones by getting them to fast from whining to begin with, for example, then no hitting or shouting, then no snacks in between meals, then no breakfast, etc… until they move on to an adult fast. There are also countless arts and crafts ideas to do with children from Ramadan decorations to advent-style calendars with pockets for treats and good deed suggestions for each day of Ramadan, to rhymes, worksheets and puzzles. Depending on where you live, there may also be lots of community initiatives set up for children from Qur'an memorization competitions and *du'a* programmes at the local mosque, to children's Ramadan workshops, and we are blessed that year on year, there is more and more available to engage our children and make the month memorable and special for them.

Sometimes, however, the bombardment of extra activities, fundraising and charity initiatives to fit in or to volunteer for on top of our regular schedules, can all be a little overwhelming. To have to think about making the kids' experience of Ramadan extra special, meaningful and memorable whilst keeping our own fasts intact, especially when parenting little ones, can sometimes feel burdensome. It is so important to get our priorities right above all else and not to lose sight of the very purpose of this holy month: fasting. As magical as we would like to make this month for our families, God Himself has explicitly highlighted to us the purpose of fasting: *'so that you may be God-conscious'*; to protect ourselves from any act of disobedience to Him. It is paramount to remember that the whole act of fasting is not to actively 'do' anything, but rather to restrain ourselves from doing certain things: eating, drinking, lying, backbiting, losing our tempers, overindulging, frivolous activities, etc.

Even if we and our children cannot fit in any extra *mustaḥabbāt* (recommended acts of worship, charity or recitation of the Qur'an), we must remember that apart from fasting and the daily *wājib ṣalāt* (obligatory prayer), everything else is a recommendation. Allah knows that fasting is itself a challenge and wants ease for us, not difficulty, He says '*Allah desires ease for you, and He does not desire for you difficulty...*' (Sūra al-Baqara 2:185). He wants us to rest and slow down, hence the rewards for simply sleeping or breathing whilst fasting. This is a time that He has designated for us to detoxify from all the spiritual toxins and bad habits we have accumulated during the year. He wants us to train our willpower muscle and recalibrate our goals, and He knows that the capacity of each one of us is different. Now is a time to reduce our regular commitments so that we can make time for *mustaḥabbāt* and conversation with our Host. We are His guests, and guests are not expected to work or to over-schedule themselves. Ultimately God wants us to perfect our fast in this month and achieve its purpose, which is first and foremost: *to do no wrong.*

أللّهُمَّ أعِنِّيْ فِيْهِ عَلَى صِيَامِهِ وَقِيَامِهِ وَجَنِّبْنِيْ فِيْهِ مِنْ هَفَوَاتِهِ وَآثَامِهِ. وَارْزُقْنِيْ فِيْهِ ذِكْرَكَ بِدَوَامِهِ بِتَوْفِيْقِكَ يَا هَادِيَ الْمُضِلِّيْنَ.

O Allah! Assist me, in this month,
to observe fast in its days and worship You in its nights;
restrain me from indulging in frivolities and transgressing (the divine
laws); keep me alive praising You throughout the month,
by Your succour, O Guide of those who are apt to go astray.

(Du'a for the 7th day of Ramadan in asking for God's help to fast properly)

>>> How are you going to ensure you keep your fast intact in this month whilst caring for your children?

>>> What one bad habit do you aim to detoxify out of your system in this holy month?

---

11. SOLITUDE AND RETREAT

وَاذْكُرْ فِيْ الْكِتَابِ مَرْيَمَ إِذِ انْتَبَذَتْ مِنْ أَهْلِهَا مَكَانًا شَرْقِيًّا.

And mention Maryam in the Book, when she retreated away from her family to an eastern place.

(Sūra Maryam 19:16)

I sat down on the sofa with my long-overdue, already-twice-warmed up cup of tea, ready to catch up on the news, maybe an episode of something on Netflix, and enjoy some alone time before my husband came back from football training. The kids were in bed and the house was finally quiet. Then, my alone time was over before it had even started.

"Mummy? Can you get me some water, please? I can't stop coughing", my youngest daughter's voice pierced through my quiet solitude.

"Mummy, can you tell her to stop coughing, please? I can't sleep", piped up the second one.

"Mummy, what's all the noise about? Why won't they just go to sleep?" bellowed my eldest.

Sigh! I am sure you too must have found yourself in the same place at some point. If our days don't start with someone's voice anxious to wake us up then they are sure to end with interruptions. For our children, there are no times when we are off limits, and for them the night does not hold sacredness as it does for us. A nightmare startles them awake. Someone wets the bed. The flu hits. What mother hasn't wished to lock herself in the bathroom for a few minutes of peace and quiet? I used to read the above verse and wish that I too could retreat away from the family to a distant, eastern land, like Lady Maryam just for a few hours.

Although Lady Maryam's circumstances were different, we can take comfort in the knowledge that even God's beloved prophets, with all their responsibilities, needed to retreat away from their people for some alone time and solitude. The Prophet (pbuh) would often go to the Cave of Hira to meditate in peace and quiet, after which he would come back rejuvenated, ready to give more of himself after having been replenished by his Lord. There is no guilt in wanting to retreat away, to need some space, some time alone. Wishing for that, but more importantly, asking for it and making time for it is healthy and essential.

Solitude, although a rare luxury for most of us, is a gift that God gives us so that we may recharge, reconnect with Him, and refill our cup (a fresh one this time!). If we don't schedule some time alone, the self-neglect and weariness can be damaging to ourselves, and also to our children. I notice that even after an hour of grocery shopping alone, or after a long bath, or stealing a few minutes of alone time here and there, I function better as a parent. Some parents, especially of young children, do not have that luxury, unfortunately, and sometimes they are so worn down that it takes a lot more than a shopping spree or a bath to get them re-energised!

For times like that, it is essential to actually schedule downtime for ourselves, bearing in mind that there are different types of downtime. A night out with the girls, a shopping trip or team sporting activity may feel energising sometimes, but at times they may drain us even further. As lovely as people's company is and as much as we are encouraged to be sociable creatures, sometimes it is God's company that we need the most. Unless our screaming schedules, messy houses, stacks of paperwork, or idle pastimes such as TV or the internet are not intentionally blocked out, we will never have time in the day to rest and receive direction from God each day.

The power of solitude, retreat and rest - even for the extroverted amongst us - cannot be undermined, and there is great benefit in enjoying your own company with God for a while and just appreciating the silence. In response to Prophet Musa (pbuh), when he asked: 'My Lord, are You far away that I should call out to You, or nearby so I can whisper to You?' God replied, 'I sit right next to the one who merely remembers Me.' Let's make sure to schedule some 'real' alone time for ourselves this week, not just for Netflix and phone calls, but to refill our cup. Use the help of babysitters and grandparents; shut off the phone, TV and laptop; ignore the dishes and paperwork to gain that solitary time for yourself.

يَا مُؤْنِسِيْ فِيْ وَحْشَتِيْ

O my best friend in my solitude!

(Extract from Du'a Jawshan al-Kabir - one of the 1000 ways to call God)

- **Do you ever feel guilty for wanting some alone time? Why do you think that is?**

- **Where in your schedule will you carve out solitude this week? Even ten minutes counts.**

- **The Prophet was purposeful about his solitude. What will you do during your me-time to truly recharge?**

12. PULLED IN ALL DIRECTIONS

رَبِّ اشْرَحْ لِيْ صَدْرِيْ وَيَسِّرْ لِيْ أَمْرِيْ

My Lord! Expand for me my breast, and make my affair easy for me.

(Sūra Ṭāhā 20:25-26)

There are times when as parents we feel pulled in all directions. Many times the demands of parenthood pull me to places I don't want to go, from getting drawn into volunteering at my daughter's summer fête, to getting yanked into having my son's friends over despite not feeling well, to getting tugged to play outside with them when really I just want to be snug indoors, to being pressured to teach a class when I have not had time to prepare properly to give it my best. Sometimes even being a participant in my yoga class feels like a stretch (no pun intended!) when the will is not there. Getting pulled around sure strains our muscles, tendons and spirit.

The difference between being pulled to do something and stretching to do something can be the difference between soreness and strength. Pulling implies resistance whereas stretching is to reach out with desire and intention. Usually a pull takes effort against something, whereas stretching is effort towards something. Even physically, the yoga stretch that elongates my calf muscle and relaxes my hamstring is very different to the movement that pulls the same muscle when I kick my son's football reluctantly in the park.

Sometimes we have no choice but to do things that we dislike, and parenthood is a taxing experience, no doubt about it. So what do we do when we feel pulled in different directions? Stretching ourselves for our children and for other people wilfully and intentionally increases our capacity, makes us more flexible, increases our range of motion and even our comfort zone. But when there is no will and no desire there, all you are left with is resistance, reluctance and even resentment.

In such situations, I have learned to ask myself: is this stretching me or pulling me? Is this facilitating for me to reach closer to God, or is it pulling me further away? Am I being pulled any closer to my own goals and pursuits as I take up these tasks, or am I simply a hamster running the wheel? Sometimes by changing our intentions and fuelling the actions with desire, we are able to turn pulls into stretches, and reach forward with our goals. Imam Ridha (pbuh) says in a beautiful hadith, *'Hearts stretch forward or pull away, and are either active or frigid. So when they stretch forward, they see and understand, and when they resist, they become dim and weary. Therefore, make the most of them when they stretch forward and are active, and leave them when they are feeble and weary.'* (Majlisī, *Biḥār al-Anwār*, v. 78, p. 353, no. 9). Sometimes we need to be selective about what we agree to and what we don't, and choose to stretch towards those actions that energise our hearts.

It amazes me that the Prophet (pbuh) was so generous with his time to people, giving them his full attention all the time, to such an extent that his critics would mock him and call him an 'ear' (*udhun*) (as mentioned in Sūra al-Tawba 9:61) because he used to listen patiently to everyone's questions and grievances, even when they would impatiently call out to him when he was in his private chambers. Allah commands people to give him space, and the Prophet (pbuh) closed all other doors that had direct access to his mosque, apart from his closest family members, so that he could continue investing time in those who would carry on his mission after him, nurturing them.

There are times when the demands pile up and we do things by sheer obligation than desire and will. Our hearts are simply not in it - they are *dim and weary*. And when we just cannot turn the things that pull us into those that stretch us positively and help us to reach our Lord, then it is time to pull away with grace and say NO to requests and invitations, whilst we continue to ask Him to increase our capacity, expand our hearts, and choose to give the best of who we are to those who need us most – our children.

اللَّهُمَّ صَلِّ عَلَى مُحَمَّد وَآلِهِ وَاقْضِ عَنِّي كُلَّمَا أَلْزَمْتَنِيهِ وَفَرَضْتَهُ عَلَيَّ لَكَ فِي وَجْه مِنْ وُجُوهِ طَاعَتِكَ،

أَوْ لِخَلْق مِنْ خَلْقِكَ وَإِنْ ضَعُفَ عَنْ ذَلِكَ بَدَنِي، وَوَهَنَتْ عَنْهُ قُوَّتِي،

وَلَمْ تَنَلْهُ مَقْدِرَتِي... فَأَدِّهِ عَنِّي مِنْ جَزِيْلِ عَطِيَّتِكَ وَكَثِيرِ مَا عِنْدَكَ، فَإِنَّكَ وَاسِعٌ كَرِيمٌ.

O Allah bless Muhammad and his household. Let me accomplish everything which You have enjoined upon me and made obligatory for me toward You, as an act of Your obedience or toward one of Your creatures, even though my body be too frail for that, my strength too feeble, my power unable to stretch to it ... Enable me to do it through Your plentiful giving and the abundance that is with You, for You are boundless and generous.

(Extract from Du'a 22 from Sahifa al-Sajjadiyya of Imam Zayn al-Abidin: his supplication during hardships that required extra effort)

- In what area of life have you been pulling instead of stretching?

- How does the definition of the two words help you to realign your goals?

- Which pulls in your life are you able to turn into stretches?

13. THREE LITTLE WORDS

وَلاَ تَقُوْلَنَّ لِشَيْءٍ إِنِّيْ فَاعِلٌ ذلِكَ غَدًا. إِلاَّ أَنْ يَشَآءَ اللهُ.

And do not say of anything: Surely I will do it tomorrow,
unless God wills it.

(Sūra al-Kahf 18:23-24)

Do you enjoy making plans for the weekend? So do I. Plans are good, except when they go awry. When I was younger, I had a hard time handling it when my meticulously laid plans would be messed up, even when they were due to factors beyond my control. In my understanding, if I was a good Muslim who did everything right, prayed on time, avoided major sins, read the Qur'an, went to mosque, helped people, I should have a smooth time in life. From young we were taught to pray 'so that' we would have a good day... pray *fajr* and your day will go well. Recite this *du'a* to get that. Make a vow to fast if you want to pass your exams. '*God, please give me x if I do y*' is an ancient refrain that people in most faith traditions are very familiar with. I'm not saying it doesn't work or that it is reprehensible, but it does reduce God to a vending machine and our acts of worship to serve *our* plans, rather than His.

As well-intentioned as our deeds may be, performed for the pleasure of Allah, it is still possible for them to be opportunistic, and for our relationship with God to be one of bartering where we *expect* Him to execute our plans for us. Although this is part of human nature, it is something we need to be wary of as Allah reminds us in the Qur'an.

The Jews in Medina would come to the Prophet and ask him various questions to challenge his knowledge. On one such occasion, they came to ask him several questions: about the fabled Sleepers of the Cave, about the nature of the *rūḥ* (Divine Spirit) and about the legendary explorer Dhul-Qarnayn. The Prophet (pbuh) would get revelation in order to be able to answer them, and so in his conviction that God would send revelation, he told the Jews that he would tell them the answer tomorrow. Tomorrow came, but the revelation did not. Nor the day after, and nor the day after that. The Prophet (pbuh) risked losing face in front of those who sought any opportunity to mock him. Finally God revealed to him to never say of anything: 'I shall do it tomorrow' without following it with 'If God wills'. Although our beloved Prophet (pbuh)'s stance came from a place of surety and conviction in God's actions, God still reminds him - and through him, us - that we, as His servants, do not have the right to *expect* the Master to do anything per our plans. He may have a different plan for us.

Of course, we are encouraged to plan ahead, to set goals for what we want, to ask fervently for whatever we desire, to beseech God, and to expect a good outcome - but not from a sense of entitlement that our deeds are deserving of it, nor because God owes us anything for those prayers and good deeds, nor even out of surety, but purely IF GOD WILLS - *in sha' Allah*.

Our children hear us saying these three little words *in sha' Allah* from very young, but have we stopped to think what we mean when we say them? The *in shā' Allah*'s that have come out of my mouth have had various shades of meaning, matching with whoever I'm talking to. If my kids ask for something and I say *in shā' Allah*, it usually means 'maybe-I'll-say-yes-but-don't-count-on-it'; when in response to 'Come over some time', it may mean 'Maybe when you invite me!' It's important to be mindful of these important three little words, because when we pass on the formula to our children, we inadvertently also pass on the nuances attached to it. Why not share the story behind *in shā' Allah* in the Qur'an with them so that they understand the significance of these three little words, as we learn to use them meaningfully, and become flexible to adjust our plans with His will, and not the other way around.

وَسَهِّلْ عَلَيْنَا مَا نَسْتَصْعِبُ مِنْ حُكْمِكَ وَأَلْهِمْنَا الاِنْقِيَادَ لِمَا أَوْرَدْتَ عَلَيْنَا مِنْ مَشِيئَتِكَ

حَتَّى لاَ نُحِبُّ تَأْخِيرَ مَا عَجَّلْتَ وَلاَ تَعْجِيلَ مَا أَخَّرْتَ...

Make easy for us what we find difficult in Your decision, and inspire us to yield to that which You bring upon us by Your will, such that we would not like to delay what You have hastened, nor hasten what You have delayed.

(Extract from Imam Zayn al-Abidin's Supplication in Asking for the Best
- no. 33 in Sahifa al-Sajjadiya)

꙳ **Be honest with yourself. How sincere has your in shā' Allah been in recent times?**

꙳ **In what specific situation will you be more mindful of your reaction to plans changing?**

14. MAKING GOD REAL

لَيْسَ كَمِثْلِهِ شَيْءٌ

There is nothing like Him

(Sūra al-Baqara 2:56)

When my son was a toddler when we were living in Iran, his favourite activity was to go through picture books of zoo animals and get me to do all their sounds, then test him to see if he could match the animals to their sounds. One afternoon, we went to visit a friend of mine at her home. While we sat sipping our tea he toddled off towards the door that opened out onto her yard where her chickens pecked and roamed about. Suddenly my son, pointing at them, cried out excitedly, 'Mummy, mummy, look! Eletant!' The jubilant look on his face was priceless as this was the first animal he was seeing up close in real life outside of a picture book, and from his perspective the scrawny Iranian chicken was an African elephant! It made me realise that our children's reality is so grounded in what they can experience with their senses and what is tangible to them. And this includes their experience of God.

When we mention God, teaching them to say Bismillah, or that this makes Allah happy, or that Allah will reward you for this or that, or teaching them that Allah is One, I always used to wonder what actually goes through their innocent, little minds. My youngest daughter, whenever I would tuck her into bed and tell her that Allah would protect her and give her good dreams, she would ask me, 'Mummy, does Allah look like you?' 'But does she have long hair like you?' 'But what colour are her eyes?' 'But won't she get tired and go to sleep?' For the longest time, she used to refer to Allah as 'she' and was convinced that Allah looked like her mum! And this is completely understandable because we are our children's first experience of God, and in a way their first objects of adoration. Making God real begins with us as parents. As mums and dads, we are their primary role models and examples as they watch and listen to us. We shape their experience of the world.

So how do we make God real to our children? The best and most powerful way is for them to see us following Him whole-heartedly and displaying godly qualities ourselves. The famous hadith of the Prophet: - 'Adopt the qualities of God' enjoins us to adopt the qualities of God. Allah is Loving (al-Wadūd) and Gentle (al-Laṭīf) so we must be loving and gentle with them. He is Compassionate (al-Raḥīm), so we must show compassion to those less fortunate than us. He is the Listener (al-Samīʿ) so we must be attentive listeners. He is the Helper (al-Muʿīn) and so we must strive to help and serve others. He is Generous and Kind (al-Karīm), and we must be kind to our children.

Before we can expect our children to see God as real, we must live out a faith that's real. This doesn't mean that we live a perfect life - none of us are capable of that other than the infallible ones. But if our life is authentic, even through the ups and downs, our children will see a mum who clings to God and His guidance more than anything else, and a dad who is ample and generous with his time and affection. Even when they grow up to develop their faith and cultivate their own relationship with God, realising that He is intangible, memories they will hold of their parents will be as 'godly'. Conversely, the opposite also holds true. When we speak of God, we are associated with Him, and if we speak of Him, but display bad behaviour, our children will become cynical about this God of ours, and potentially disassociate themselves, as the children and descendants of Prophet Yaʿqub refer to Him as 'Your God and the God of your forefathers' (Sūra al-Baqara 2:133) in their nonchalance.

As we live out an active and vibrant faith in our homes that is not confined to the mosque or to special occasions, we help the invisible and intangible God of adults become real for our children. It is only when *we* worship God consciously at home that our children will know who this 'Allah' is.

أَللّٰهُمَّ اجْعَلْنِيْ أَخْشَاكَ كَأَنِّيْ أَرَاكَ، وَأَسْعِدْنِيْ بِتَقْوَاكَ، وَلَا تُشْقِنِيْ بِمَعْصِيَتِكَ ...

O Allah, let me be in awe of You as if I am seeing You, and make me successful through being conscious of You, and do not make me wretched as a result of disobeying You...

(Extract from Du'a 'Arafa taught by Imam Husayn (pbuh))

᪥ **Do you remember any of your parents' conscious interaction with God as a child, or mentioning Him in daily life?**

᪥ **How did these impact you as a child, and then as an adult?**

᪥ **What is one way that you could make God 'real' for your children?**

_____

_____

_____

_____

_____

15. GATHER AROUND THE TABLE

قَالَ عِيْسَى ابْنُ مَرْيَمَ أَللهُمَّ رَبَّنَا أَنْزِلْ عَلَيْنَا مَآئِدَةً مِنَ السَّمَاءِ تَكُوْنُ لَنَا عِيْدًا لِأَوَّلِنَا وَآخِرِنَا وَآيَةً مِنْكَ وَارْزُقْنَا وَأَنْتَ خَيْرُ الرَّازِقِيْنَ.

'Isa, son of Maryam, said, 'O God, our Sustainer! Send down to us a table spread from heaven, which will be a source of celebration for the first and last of us, and a sign from You. And grant us provision for You are the best of providers.

(Sūra al-Mā'ida [The Table] 5:114)

My new table is already a year old, having replaced a well-worn, old, hand-me-down. In that year, despite my best efforts to keep it new, to use a tablecloth, and coasters with hot drinks, and wipe it down after dinner, it quickly took on bumps, bruises and scratches. Even water marks and unexplained stickiness! I keep having to remind myself, however, that a table is meant to be used and that these imperfections are signs that it is more than just a piece of furniture. It tends to be our home base, stacked with school books, stationery and mail; at times used as an art easel, then later on the place where we eat.

For us, as for many families I am sure, the table is far more than that. It is a place where we gather, a sacred space where no phones or digital devices are allowed. It is the one place where we communally sit to eat together at least once a day, talk, bounce ideas off each other, laugh, have family meetings and share life together. The table accommodates all of us together, where we're all relaxed and everyone comes willingly to be fed and nourished.

There is very special and unparalleled benefit in eating together, which is why even if humans feel perfectly comfortable living alone, it always feels a little uncomfortable to eat all by oneself (hence the urge to switch on the TV when eating alone). The viral South Korean phenomenon of Mukbang that has gained so much popularity on Youtube is great evidence of this. People order and eat large amounts of food live in front of their webcams whilst an audience of people watch them live online. Psychologists and anthropologists have concluded that its origins lie in the loneliness, anxiety and unhappiness that Koreans face in their increasingly individualistic society, especially because eating has always been an inherently social activity in their culture. Eating a meal alone just does not feel right to them, so sadly they resort to Mukbang.

Imam Zayn al-Abidin (pbuh) when donating food to hungry people in the street, would actually dismount and sit down to eat with them on the floor, giving them company. Far more than just furniture, a table or *sufra* is a sacred space. In Madagascar, where I grew up, whenever food would be served at the mosque, instead of one long, rectangular *sufra* being laid with people sitting in rows either side of it, we would gather in groups of 8 to 10 around a large, round, metal tray balancing on a stand. The food would be piled in the middle in a big mound - usually rice and curry - and everyone would partake together from the same tray, eating from the side closest to them, usually with their hands. There was no need for individual crockery and cutlery, and it made for great conversation with young and old around our makeshift table on the floor.

In the verse above, and in many accounts of paradise mentioned in supplications, there are often references to banquets or tables laden with the finest foods and fruits in abundance. In that heavenly dimension communal gathering, friendship, laughter, belonging and deep family bonds will be eternal. The table that Prophet Isa's disciples asked him to request from God was a little slice of heaven, to be enjoyed and gathered around, to entertain guests and nourish bodies and souls. Our tables too can be exactly that.

الْحَمْدُ للهِ الَّذِيْ أَطْعَمَنِيْ وَسَقَانِيْ، وَرَزَقَنِيْ وَرَبَّانِيْ، وَجَعَلَنِيْ مِنَ الْمُسْلِمِيْنَ.

All praise be to the One who fed me and quenched me, provided me and nourished me, and made me among those who submit to Him.

(Supplication recommended after eating a meal)

- ❯❯❯ How often do you and your family gather at the table or sufra?

- ❯❯❯ What keeps you from gathering as often as you'd like?

- ❯❯❯ What could you do to transform your table into more than just a piece of furniture?

_____

_____

_____

_____

_____

_____

_____

16. HELP IS AT HAND

مَتَى نَصْرُ اللهِ ۚ أَلَآ إِنَّ نَصْرَ اللهِ قَرِيْبٌ.

...when will the help of God come? Now surely the help of God is near.

(Sūra al-Baqara 2:214)

More times than I choose to remember, when my children were younger (and so was I), I often felt frazzled, overwhelmed and even a little bit annoyed with the juggling act that I was to perform round-the-clock, especially when it came to picking and dropping the children to different activities, or birthday parties at opposite ends of town, or managing work and house while the kids were sick. Becoming frazzled and overwhelmed is absolutely normal, and the job of raising little humans necessarily leaves us feeling that way due to the sheer enormity of the task, but my annoyance was of my own doing. In that state of helplessness, I would often feel that God should be helping me. I was raising children, at times as a single parent, and doing my very best, and in times of need it just didn't seem that God's help was anywhere in sight.

In answer to my exasperated sighs of: 'When is this going to get easier, God? When are You going to help me?' He tells us himself in the Qur'an, in the verse above, that the help of God is near! The beautiful thing about the word *qarīb* in Arabic is that it encompasses both time and place, so the same phrase: *inna naṣr Allāhi qarīb* means that God's help will come soon, but it also means that God's help is at hand nearby. Whilst waiting impatiently for some magical help to come down from the sky, I often neglected to understand that God's help could take many forms and was available right at my doorstep, if only I would reach for it. So I learned many years ago that if I needed help, I had to ask God for it, but also reach out for it, and that it's an utter myth to think that any mum can do and be all things, all of the time.

It is okay to ask for help. It is not a weakness to need the help of a spouse, friend, in-laws or neighbours. God has gifted us with these people for a reason, and the adage that it takes a village to raise a child drips with wisdom. I recently came to learn the Xhosa/Zulu term 'ubuntu' which I love! It literally means 'I am, because you are', in that a person functions as a person through other people. Ubuntu is that nebulous concept of common humanity and compassion. God has blessed us with one another, and with ubuntu between us, to help carry the difficult and heavy burdens that different seasons bring. In fact, I have come to realise that the majority of the time, it has been my own pride that has kept others away from my need, and deep down my annoyance is at my own self for failing to ask for it. I don't have to be a supermum or to seem like I have it all together. Asking for help does not mean that I don't have it all together anyway!

So now if this means asking my sisters or parents to babysit, or asking a neighbour to pick up a few groceries when she goes to Costco, or a football dad to give my son a lift back, I don't hesitate. The beautiful side-effect that results from asking others for help is that it makes people feel needed and useful to others. My tribe around me are a lovely bunch, fully in sync with ubuntu (even though they may not even have heard of the word!), and all I have to do is ask and they not only help out, but are grateful to have been asked! Best of all, it opens the door for others to feel comfortable enough to ask for my help whenever they need it.

When we sincerely ask for God's help, it may well come in human form, not necessarily landing in our lap but for us to reach towards: healthcare professionals, counsellors, handymen, mechanics, financial advisors, cleaners, IT technicians, authors of parenting books, and general support. The recent rise of helpful community groups online is a reminder that humans need help, and that although God's help comes in all shapes and forms, it is always nearby.

... يَا نَاصِرَ مَنِ اسْتَنْصَرَهُ ... يَا صَرِيخَ مَنِ اسْتَصْرَخَهُ، يَا مُعِينَ مَنِ اسْتَعَانَهُ، يَا مُغِيثَ مَنِ اسْتَغَاثَهُ

O Helper of whoever asks for His help... O cry of whoever cries out to Him, O Helper of whoever appeals to Him, O Rescuer of whoever beseeches to Him

(Extract from Du'a Jawshan al-Kabīr, Part 30)

- What kinds of help do you wish you could ask for?

- If, like me, you struggle to ask for help, what do you think could be the reason behind that?

- If you aren't in a season of great need right now, how might you be of help to other mums?

17. PRENATAL STRESS

فَأَجَاءَهَا الْمَخَاضُ إِلَى جِذْعِ النَّخْلَةِ قَالَتْ يَا لَيْتَنِيْ مِتُّ قَبْلَ هذَا وَكُنْتُ نَسْيًا مَنْسِيًّا.

فَنَادَاهَا مِنْ تَحْتِهَا أَلاَّ تَحْزَنِيْ قَدْ جَعَلَ رَبُّكِ تَحْتَكِ سَرِيًّا.

And the throes of childbirth compelled her to hold on to the trunk of palm tree. She said, 'O how I wish I had died before this and had been a thing quite forgotten'.
Then (the child) called out to her from beneath her, 'Do not be upset, surely your Lord has made a stream flow beneath you.'

(Sūra Maryam 19:23-24)

What old wives previously only speculated about, that babies were affected by maternal stress levels whilst in the womb, have now been researched and verified by science. Negative emotions such as increased levels of stress, anger, being upset and unhappy for a long time, being intensely frightened, jealous or resentful have all been shown to affect both the mother and her unborn child. The surge of cortisol and other stress hormones passes into the blood, which are then conveyed to the baby through the placenta.

Research now indicates that stress in the earlier stages of pregnancy may result in physical abnormalities, while stress in the later stages of pregnancy results in behavioural changes. Emotional disturbances in mothers have also been linked to babies who are irritable, cry excessively or have feeding problems, though this is by no means the only contributing factor. Although it may not be possible to remain entirely stress-free for nine months, a mother should try to avoid stress as much as possible, especially prolonged stress. Obviously maternal stress is not the be-all and end-all of our children's future wellbeing, and it is certainly not the only thing by far that is going to affect how our children turn out, but it does have some effect (amongst many others).

The Qur'anic verse above quotes Lady Maryam and how anxious she feels whilst she is all alone in the last stages of her pregnancy. She had cause to feel anxious and upset, having had to leave her family at God's behest, knowing what ridicule and derision she would face at the hands of the community, and not knowing how she would handle it all. She actually wishes she was dead and that everyone would just forget about her existence. And her baby calls out and tells her not be upset, reassuring her that God had made a stream of soothing water flow beneath her that would ease her pain!

It is natural to feel anxious over a process that we have little control over and that is reputed to be painful. We are lucky to be living in an age where we are able to hear our baby's heartbeat, see ultrasound images, and have access to healthcare and information right at our fingertips throughout gestation. And whilst it's important to use the information we have to prepare us, to have a birthing plan, to know our options for pain relief, etc. there can be such a thing as information overload. Whilst pregnant with my first baby, I was living abroad for most of my pregnancy with little Internet connectivity, and no British pregnancy magazines at hand. I felt relatively relaxed having read books about gestation and labour. During my second though, back in London, I perused countless pregnancy magazines with all their sensationalist and horrifying birthing stories of everything that could possibly go wrong, of course designed to hook people in to buy more! And naturally, I felt anxious towards the end.

Being selective about the kind of reading material and the kind of sensory stimuli we expose ourselves to whilst pregnant is essential. Now is not the time to engage in and get worked up about depressing politics, now is not the time to watch all the bad news about rising crime levels and feel sad ALL the time. On the contrary, using this time to do things that engender positive feelings in us, and that produce a natural high are so beneficial: things like charity work, helping people, connecting with God, watching motivational talks, learning about the lives of great humanitarians with noble qualities, spending time in nature, listening to and reading Qur'an. We must activate the same feelings in us, of calm and positivity, that we would want our children to grow up with. One of my mentors in Iran even went as far as telling me not to look at rubbish dumps or car accidents in the street, and to avoid the company of people who were irritating or especially those who were in the habit of gossiping or backbiting, and anything that could potentially distress me.

Those of us who are already parents will be able to vouch (in hindsight!) that giving birth is not all pain. For me the experience was as close as I have ever got to understanding God's verse 'Indeed **with** difficulty is ease'. **With**, i.e. right alongside it. With every contraction, we facilitate and ease baby's passage into the world, and our own status is increased, our sins wiped away. Allah is *al-Qābiḍ* (The One who contracts things) as well as *al-Bāsiṭ* (The One who expands them) at the same time. It is not just my baby being born, but my own birth into this world as a mother. You will never be the same person again.

Ultimately conception, gestation and delivery are all tremendous exercises in trust. We are not in control of a whole lot, and yet we are in control of significant aspects. Our babies' time in our wombs do have a bearing on the rest of their lives - but that too, paradoxically, is not something we can perceive, sense or feel happening. The entire process of creation we are not witness to, as God says: 'I did not make them witnesses of the creation of the heavens and the earth, and nor of the creation of their own selves.' (Sūra al-Kahf 18:51) - we are mere onlookers trying to do our best and ultimately place ALL our trust in God. What is in our control is to be committed to looking after ourselves, to have good *halal* food in abundance, to avoid feeling sad and upset, to feel safe and not endangered, and to do lots of *du'a*.

رَبِّ هَبْ لِيْ مِنْ لَدُنْكَ ذُرِّيَّةً طَيِّبَةً إِنَّكَ سَمِيْعُ الدُّعَاء.

My Lord, grant me from Yourself wholesome offspring. Indeed You are the Hearer of supplication

(Sūra Āl 'Imran 3:38 - Prophet Zakariyya's supplication
for a good, wholesome child)

➤ **If you are expecting, what steps will you take to reduce stress and anxiety levels during your pregnancy?**

➤ **What other times in your life have you had to completely surrender control and trust in God?**

_____

_____

_____

_____

_____

_____

_____

_____

18. POST-NATAL SPIRITUAL BLUES

وَإِذَا سَأَلَكَ عِبَادِيْ عَنِّيْ فَإِنِّيْ قَرِيْبٌ أُجِيْبُ دَعْوَةَ الدَّاعِيْ إِذَا دَعَانِ
فَلْيَسْتَجِيْبُوْا لِيْ وَلْيُؤْمِنُوْا بِيْ لَعَلَّهُمْ يَرْشُدُوْنَ.

*And when My servants ask you about me, Indeed I am near! I answer
the call of the caller when he calls me, so let them respond to me and
believe in me so that they may be rightly guided.*

(Sūra al-Baqara 2:186)

Post-natal depression is a very real and very scary thing, caused
by the sudden plummeting of pregnancy hormones and a change in
chemicals in the brain, in addition to the sleepless nights, uncertainty
in handling a tiny human being without an instruction manual, and
a whole host of other factors. That is, however, a topic I shall leave to
expert guidance, coupled with support from family and friends, as it
is a serious condition that warrants professional help. I was very lucky
not to have suffered from it, unlike many others who do, but what I
did go through was a big, fat, spiritual vacuum postpartum after my
first, very colicky baby. Having prayed all my prayers on time for
nine months with no break, recited pages and pages of Qur'an, done
as many *mustaḥabbāt* as I could in preparation for my baby, along
with him had come sleepless nights and physical exhaustion. I felt
half-dead, groggily just managing to make *fajr* on time, let alone the
extra *duʿas* or *dhikr*. My Qur'an recitation was reduced to a short *sūra*
or two read on my baby for protection, and mosque-going was a thing
of the past. Everything had changed and yet I was to remain on top of
it all, to ooze out positive energy for the sake of my child and my milk.
I was feeling disconnected from the very Source of my great blessing,
only able to fit in the bare minimum *wājib* acts. I knew I wasn't alone

in feeling this way as many of my friends found themselves spiritually depleted too.

If you too are feeling this way, take heart! God has purposely bent the rules a little for women and excused them from certain things. Apart from the obligatory, he has made everything else *mustahabb* and secondary to looking after her children; neither is it necessary for her to earn her livelihood, nor attend Friday or congregational prayers outside of her home. It is all part of His mercy towards us that He has designated a mother's reward for waking up in the middle of the night to being like one who stays awake the whole night in vigil in Jihad, or the sheer number of rewards accorded to her for every drop of milk she feeds, or how our slate is wiped clean when we give birth. All these clues point to the very poignant fact that God does not expect us to get closer to Him via the same means we used to pre-motherhood. He has promoted us to the status of motherhood and a different type of spirituality that comes with the territory. Our children are now the new means by which we get closer to Him. So instead of seeking a way to perform ritual acts or pray in spite of our children, or to side-step them in an effort to reconnect with Allah, we are to involve them and seek a way to God through them.

This also shows us that we can derive strength and energy from the *wājib* acts themselves. Even if the bare minimum is all we can manage, then we must make that count by letting it be our very best. We can see that *wājib salat* as a time-out, take deep breaths, and make the whole experience last; pour out our hearts to God in *sajda*, regaining strength for the next part of the day. As for the extra *du'as*, remember that they are *mustahabb* and primarily designed to teach us how to articulate our own wants to God in our own words. He says in the verse above: 'Surely I am near, and I answer the call of the caller whenever he calls Me'. The caller. Not the worshipper, not the supplicant, not the pious devotee, not the one who is fluent at reciting in Arabic, but *whoever* calls out to Him. The best call is that which flows from the heart and onto the tongue. That is the very best way to maintain the closeness and connection with God - to speak to Him directly and ask Him for every little thing: the strength, the energy, the colic to stop, the milk to flow, the baby to sleep, the child to be righteous, and so on ...

We know that when done with the intention of seeking the pleasure of Allah, every little act in their upbringing becomes an act of worship, as the very concept of worship in Islam is not restricted to acts of ritual worship. Possibly the greatest thing a mother can do to fuel herself to bring up her children on the right path and for the growth of her own soul is to be connected to Allah through her voice, in calling out to him throughout her day.

يَا سَرِيْعَ الرِّضَى اِغْفِرْ لِمَنْ لاَ يَمْلِكُ إِلاَّ الدُّعَاءَ.

يَا مَن اِسْمُهُ دَوَاءٌ، وَذِكْرُهُ شِفَاءٌ، وَطَاعَتُهُ غِنَى...

O the one who is readily pleased, forgive the one who owns nothing but his calling out!

O He whose Name is a remedy and whose remembrance is a cure, and obedience to Him is enriching.

(Extract from Du'a Kumayl – taught by Imam Ali (pbuh) to his companion Kumayl Ibn Ziyad)

يﺮﻣ **In what ways could you ensure that your *wājib* acts energise you?**

يﺮﻣ **How could you activate your special maternal voice to express your most pressing needs to God during your day?**

19. SIBLING LOVE AND LOATHING

إِذْ قَالُوا لَيُوسُفُ وَأَخُوهُ أَحَبُّ إِلَى أَبِينَا مِنَّا وَنَحْنُ عُصْبَةٌ إِنَّ أَبَانَا لَفِيْ ضَلَالٍ مُبِينٍ. اقْتُلُوا يُوسُفَ أَوِ اطْرَحُوهُ أَرْضًا يَخْلُ لَكُمْ وَجْهُ أَبِيكُمْ وَتَكُونُوا مِنْ بَعْدِهِ قَوْمًا صَالِحِينَ.

When they said, 'Surely Yusuf and his brother are dearer to our father than [the rest of] us, though we are a hardy group. Our father is indeed in manifest error. Kill Yusuf or cast him away into some [distant] land, so that your father's love may be exclusively yours, and that you may become a righteous lot after that.'

(Sūra Yusuf 12: 8-9)

One of the very first associated words that jumps to mind when the word 'sibling' is mentioned is the word 'rivalry'. Whether it is because we have all been through it, or because we witness it daily in our own children, this is a clue in itself that it is a very natural part of growing up. Children - who are animalistic and territorial by nature - have to share the same set of parents, toys, house, and living space. In actual fact, most sibling relationships are no less complicated than marriages, since neither do we get to choose our siblings, nor can they be divorced, and yet they outlast most marriages!

One of the first stories in the Qur'an after the story of our creation is that of Habil and Qabil, where Qabil in his uncontrollable jealousy towards his brother, ends up killing him. Jealousy between siblings is very much a reality and it is not abnormal for children to feel jealous of one another. The aim of parents should be to control it and keep it within appropriate limits. It cannot be totally eliminated. The Qur'an also gives us the example of Prophet Yusuf and his brothers, where they thought that their father loved him more than he loved them. The verse above clearly expresses the cause of their contention: 'that your father's love may be exclusively yours' (Sūra Yusuf 12:9), and indeed the cause of most sibling antagonism is: perceived loss of parental love! Children wish to have the greatest share of their parents love and attention. When siblings take it away from them, even temporarily, it becomes greatly upsetting. Only time and maturity helps the child understand that this loss is only imagined and not real.

Sometimes, parental love may have nothing to do with it, but children will find something or the other to taunt each other with or bicker about. I remember from my own childhood playing beautifully with my sisters one minute and being in a fierce verbal contest for the most cutting come-backs the next, whilst my mum's sanity was at stake trying to make sense of who said what to whom first, in her bid to be as fair as possible! Within minutes we would be back to being friends upstairs while my poor mother was left stewing for hours over how she could solve our disputes, oblivious to our restored peace, albeit short-lived! For a parent, it is very unsettling to have two or more parts of yourself constantly at each other's throats on their childhood journey.

There are seemingly two camps of parents out there: those who venture knee-deep into aiming to solve every dispute at the risk of premature senility and high blood pressure; and those who walk away saying; 'Unless there is blood, fire or something broken, I don't want to hear about it', at the risk of shutting out real cries for help from a child being constantly victimised. We, through the sunnah of the Prophet (pbuh) and his family, take the middle path. There are a myriad of skills, strategies and tips out there to help us nurture our children's sibling relationships, but here we'll focus specifically on the wise principles that Islam teaches us about how to effectively manage our children. Their wisdom is divine and practical, not theoretical or man-made. Bearing these in mind and a light-hearted attitude on our shoulders, there are many things we can do to prevent jealousy between siblings and to nip it in the bud when they are still young, to handle it and manage it effectively when they are older, and to foster deep and lasting bonds between our offspring:

1) JUSTICE or EQUALITY: This is probably the most important quality for a parent to have when dealing with their children, as it is the parents who set the scene for how the children will behave with each other. Aim to treat each child as an individual, taking into account, age, gender and birth order. The Prophet (pbuh) always encouraged his companions to treat their children with justice, saying, 'Maintain justice among your children in gifts, just like you would like them to be just with you in goodness and affection.' The equality should be there in the act of giving them gifts that no one is left out, but justice is maintained when each child is given according to what is suitable for his age, gender and needs.

It is very important to give them equal attention and affection, regardless of their birth order, gender or age. Imam Ali (pbuh) narrated, *'The Prophet saw a man with two sons, who kissed one of them but made the other one feel left out, so the Prophet (pbuh) said, 'Why do you not treat both of them equally?!'* Of course this doesn't mean that every time you hug one child, you have to hug all the rest in turn, as this would ruin the significance of the hug for the child who originally needed it, but it means that each child should feel regular and real affection from his or her parents, and should not feel left out, especially when everyone is together, either through inside jokes, snide remarks or displays of affection for another child to the exclusion of himself.

Don't create unnecessary rivalry by labelling, comparing, or casting children in roles, such as 'She's the tidy one, but he just always manages to get so dirty', or showing favouritism, even if the differences between the two are really marked. A bit of rivalry can be healthy, but must not be initiated by the parents where a child should feel that he will only be respected by his parents if he makes the same grades as the other or scores like his brother. Fierce competitiveness can be avoided by nurturing their individual talents and accepting that every child is unique and different. Comparing children is the single biggest parental contributor to sibling rivalry.

2) GENDER DIFFERENCES: Again, western parenting methods these days overemphasise that boys and girls be treated the same, or that everything from toys to clothing should be gender-neutral. But there are many studies done to show the detriment of this. Islam has honoured women from when they are little girls, but it is us who deny them the respect they are due. The Prophet (pbuh) said, '*He who goes to the market and buys a gift to take back to his family is as one who is taking charity to a group of needy people. He should begin (giving gifts) to the female members of his family before the males.*' Instil from a young age that ladies go first, and girls get presents first. If they are all the same gender, then we start from the youngest. There is wisdom in all of this and if we set Islamic principles as the ground rules, this facilitates our life so our children know their natural place and don't become bone-pickers and fight over every chocolate chip of every cookie.

3) BIRTH ORDER: These days a lot of attention is given by psychologists, authors of parenting books, and even parents themselves to birth order as being a negative contributing factor. Birth order certainly does not *cause* sibling rivalry but it can provoke it if parents label their children according to their birth order and favour them based on that. Islam teaches us to honour their birth order. The oldest has a very defined role, especially if it's a boy. He holds responsibility for his younger siblings on his shoulders, especially in his parents' absence, but they in turn are to respect him. If we nurture such a role in a positive way in our households, we will find that it will be the glue that holds our children together when they're older, and when the generation gap has widened even more, and parents can no longer keep up with their children. I know from experience that when I tell my eldest daughter: 'Remind your sister to pray her ṣalāt, please', then she herself will see to it that she prays, ensuring of course

her own *ṣalāt* in the process! Modern Western methods refute this, saying that it causes resentment in the other siblings, but this is only when parents go to extremes, labelling and comparing them. When we nurture respectful sibling relationships where the younger ones have to respect the older ones, and they in turn have to look after the younger ones, it leads to mutual respect, an interdependence between them, and a lighter load on the parents.

4) ṢILAT AL-RAḤIM: Above all, endeavour to be a living example of sibling harmony with your own brothers and sisters. Our actions have a much greater impact on children than the best-phrased lectures. Witnessing family feuds, family ties being broken, and silent treatments between uncles and aunts are not going to leave a very good impression on their minds.

5) NURTURE THEIR RELATIONSHIP: by celebrating Sibling Day! Why not? There's Mother's Day, Father's Day, World Beard Day and even Go Barefoot Day. Pick any day in the year, preferably a month which is empty of birthdays or other celebrations. Take each child shopping separately for gifts for each other. Have decorations, ice cream, cake, and a party where they all promise to always love each other and take care of each other. The Prophet (pbuh) said, *'A gift brings about affection, reinforces brotherhood, and removes grudges. Give gifts to each other and you will love each other.'*

There are probably as many tips and strategies for nurturing sibling harmony as there are parents out there, each with their own particular method, but the important thing to remember is to stay calm, relaxed and patient with them, and to resort to the Maker and His divine strategies for optimal functioning of His creatures. Sometimes nothing may work and we may have to admit that perhaps the thing we are fighting so hard to remedy and to prevent is actually there for a reason. In the animal kingdom, fighting between siblings prepares them for adulthood, to learn to live with other more hostile animals in the pack, and develops muscle tone, courage, and confidence.

Even with human 'cubs', it prepares them for many an unpleasant relationship in the future, as well as teaching them negotiating and problem-solving skills. All praise be to Allah, our Wise and Nurturing Creator who fashioned us in this unique way!

رَبِّ اغْفِرْ لِيْ وَلِأَخِيْ وَأَدْخِلْنَا فِيْ رَحْمَتِكَ وَأَنْتَ أَرْحَمُ الرَّاحِمِيْنَ

My Lord! Forgive me and my brother and admit us into Your mercy,
for You are the most Merciful of all merciful ones.

(Sūra al-A'rāf 7:151 - Prophet Musa's supplication for himself and his brother, Prophet Haroon)

- How did your own parents handle any sibling rivalry or bickering in your household?

- If your children's constant bickering is a challenge for you, what could you do differently with them today?

20. EVE (حَوّاء)

يَآ أَيُّهَا النَّاسُ اتَّقُوْا رَبَّكُمُ الَّذِيْ خَلَقَكُمْ مِنْ نَفْسٍ وَاحِدَةٍ وَخَلَقَ مِنْهَا

زَوْجَهَا وَبَثَّ مِنْهُمَا رِجَالاً كَثِيْرًا وَنِسَآءً...

*O people! Be conscious of your duty to God Who created you from a
single being and created its mate from the same, and spread from these
two many men and women...*

(Sūra al-Nisāʾ 4:1)

Whilst the Qurʾan details the story of our original parents Adam
and Eve in many places, it does not actually mention her by name.
We know her name was Hawwa, meaning 'source of life', from the
Prophetic traditions. There is also no mention in the Qurʾan of her
having been created from his left rib or from clay leftover from when
God made Adam. What it does mention is that He created her so that
Adam may find tranquillity in her and that they both lived happily
in the Garden, until their fall to earth. There is also no mention in
the Qurʾan of her having been guileful, or having deceived Adam or
of having been the first to eat from the tree. Every single mention is
of the two of them together: both were told not to approach the tree
or listen to Shaytan, but he enticed them both together. They both
ate from the tree, both felt ashamed, both called out to God, and he
forgave them both. The Qurʾan, unlike the Biblical tradition, does not
see sin, suffering and pain as something that we have inherited from
Eve, but as something that is the very nature of this disorderly, chaotic,
material world of cause and effect. Our task then, is to constantly find
Him within the chaos, the suffering and sin, as Adam and Eve did.

Hadiths further describe to us that they were sent down to earth, probably to Makka at the Mountain of Mercy, from which they went on to Muzdalifa and the actual Sanctuary (*haram*). They missed their blissful time in the Garden, especially worshipping Allah with the throngs of angels, and beseeched Him as to what they could do now on earth. Angel Jibra'il came down and marked out the place directly below their original place of worship and *tawaf* up in the heavens, and asked him to build a place of worship for himself and his progeny. It is said that Adam and Eve were separated: he was on a hill called Safa and she was on another called Marwa, and they missed each other terribly. Before he was allowed to go and see her, he had to first groom himself: cut his hair and nails, which we do until this day during *hajj* in following in his footsteps. They had had distance from each other to contend with as well as distance from their Beloved.

Unfortunately we don't know much about our first mother, as a person, but we are told to think about their story, mentioned numerous times in the Qur'an, to piece them together and to reflect. What were her thoughts at having been deceived by Shaytan? At having been expelled from the beautiful Garden? Did she enjoy this world with all it had to offer when previously they had known neither space, nor time, nor heat, nor cold, nor hunger, nor thirst, nor shame, nor pain? How did she deal with the physical pain of childbirth without the experience of human mothers and sisters before her, and no antenatal classes or pregnancy magazines? What about the emotional anguish when one of her sons murders the other? How did she process that grief? At least she didn't have the 'Joneses' and 'what will people say' to contend with - but even then, how does one process grief like that without the support of a human community or people who can share past experience? Such big feelings, so much trauma, grief and pain! I don't claim to have the answers, but I'm certain that if their greatest pain on earth was separation from the Beloved, then certainly God would have been her first and only resort.

As the original and first mother, what motherly advice would she have imparted to us, her children? I think she would have passed on the same wisdom that God taught them upon their descent to earth, and that they learned from their mistakes:

"Resort to God, my child. This beautiful, green world - although pleasant to look at -, is difficult. There is blood and pain, hunger and heat, and dry skin. It is hard enough to birth children but to raise them to be God-conscious, that is even more challenging. This world is temporary though[1], so keep your chin up, and aspire for nothing less than the Garden. Follow His guidance and you will have nothing to fear or be sad about[2]. And in addition to all the leaves, fur and feathers we've been using to cover ourselves with, the cloak of God-consciousness, that is the best[3]. Stay away from Shaytan, my child, and treat him as an enemy. Do not be deceived by Him[4]. And whenever you slip up or wrong yourself, just repent sincerely and He will forgive you[5]. He is our Sustainer, our Nourisher, our Cave. Space and time are but an illusion of this world - He is near, so keep resorting back to Him."

---

1. Sūra al-Tawba 9:38 – "The provision of this world's life compared to the Hereafter is but little."

2. Sūra al-Baqara 2:38 - "We said, 'Get down from it all of you; and surely there will come to you guidance from Me, then whoever follows My guidance, no fear shall come upon them nor shall they grieve'."

3. Sūra al-Aʿrāf 7:26 - "O children of Adam! We have indeed sent down to you clothing to cover your shame and for adornment, and the clothing that protects against evil, that is the best."

4. Sūra al-Fāṭir 35:6 - "Surely Shaytan is an enemy for you, so treat him as an enemy!"

5. Sūra al-Baqara 2:58 - "...prostrate and say words of repentance. We will forgive you your sins, and we will increase the reward for those who do good."

رَبَّنَا ظَلَمْنَا أَنْفُسَنَا وَإِنْ لَمْ تَغْفِرْ لَنَا وَتَرْحَمْنَا لَنَكُوْنَنَّ مِنَ الْخَاسِرِيْنَ.

"Our Lord! We have both wronged ourselves, and if You do not forgive us and have mercy on us, We will certainly be of the losers."

(Sūra al-Aʻrāf 7:23 - Adam and Hawwa's repentance after they ate from the tree)

〰️ **What are some practical ways you could implement one or two points from 'Eve's motherly advice'?**

〰️ **How do you feel you have benefitted from other people's past experiences and mistakes in your life?**

21. DOING IT ALONE

رَبَّنَا إِنِّيْ أَسْكَنْتُ مِنْ ذُرِّيَّتِيْ بِوادٍ غَيْرِ ذِيْ زَرْعٍ عِنْدَ بَيْتِكَ الْمُحَرَّم
رَبَّنَا لِيُقِيْمُوا الصَّلَاةَ فَاجْعَلْ أَفْئِدَةً مِنَ النَّاسِ تَهْوِيْ إِلَيْهِمْ وارْزُقْهُمْ
مِنَ الثَّمَرَاتِ لَعَلَّهُمْ يَشْكُرُوْنَ.

*O our Lord! Surely I have settled part of my offspring in a barren
valley near Your Sacred House, our Lord, that they may keep up the
prayer. Therefore, make the hearts of people incline towards them and
provide them with fruits, so that they may be grateful.*

(Sūra Ibrahim 14:37)

My social media feed, populated with parenting blogs (of course),
periodically brings up articles, blog posts and vlogs, where new parents
– mums and dads - concede that parenthood is the single most difficult
thing that they've ever had to deal with, and how becoming a parent
is a challenge that stands in a league of its own, more overwhelming
and stressful than any other career or job. I am sure this is something
that all parents agree with at some point in their lives. Bringing up
strong-willed little humans in all their loudness and clumsiness with
their own talents and personalities to discover and nurture, is no easy
feat, requiring maybe more than just one village to raise them! We've
all felt it at times, even with the support of a community around us.

More often than not, however, the experience that many, many
mothers live daily is far from the idyllic image of well-supported
parents raising their broods altogether. So many mothers are doing
it alone, whether officially as single parents, or simply feeling all
alone in that mammoth task. One does not have to look far within a
community to find:

⁂ a widowed mother of young children, recently been bereaved, forlornly missing her husband and hoping to see glimpses of his character in her children;

⁂ a newly-divorced mother, navigating the quagmire of legal terms and bureaucracy in her mind, whilst trying to act upbeat and cheerful for her kids, despite her mental exhaustion;

⁂ a mother having to play the roles of Mum and Dad, and good cop bad cop combined, when just Mum on its own is a hard enough job;

⁂ a mother having to make tough decisions about schooling, discipline, social media, boundaries, privileges, and pocket money without the input of a significant other;

⁂ a mother who has parented alone for so long now that she no longer remembers or knows an alternative feeling besides that;

⁂ a mother handling a whole household by herself: the finances, insurance, household maintenance, motoring, health and emergencies without a sounding board or anyone to delegate to;

⁂ a single mother of little ones, desperate for another pair of hands when her one child wakes up in the middle of the night screaming with earache whilst she holds her other one vomiting in the bathroom, praying the third one doesn't wake up too;

⁂ a mother of a wayward teen who can't share her crippling fears and anxieties for his future with anyone for fear of being judged;

⁂ a single mother, hit with melancholy as soon as her children go to bed, craving male companionship, but constantly oscillating between swearing off re-marriage 'for the sake of the kids' and wanting to remarry 'for the sake of the kids';

ᗑᎀ a married 'single' mother whose husband works away for most of the year, not having him there to fight her corner and support her when her children answer back and question her authority;

ᗑᎀ a mother hit with a deep sense of loneliness on a Sunday morning, urging her children to play quietly from the crack of dawn, as her husband sleeps in until noon;

ᗑᎀ a single mother who knows deep down that no amount of kicking a ball and playing video games with her son will compensate for the absence of a male role model in the home;

ᗑᎀ a mother who craves proper adult conversation and mental stimulation besides feeding, potty-training and playgroups;

ᗑᎀ and a mother who may as well be single-parenting given the minimal input from her alleged 'co-parent'.

This is neither a new phenomenon, nor a new struggle, nor even a new loneliness. This may well have been the struggle of Aamina, the widowed mother of Prophet Muhammad (pbuh), or of Hajar, the ostracised single mother of Prophet Isma'il (pbuh) in a strange land, or of Lady Maryam, the single mother of Prophet Isa (pbuh). These women are heroines, united in their struggle of bringing up good, Muslim children on their own. And the life of a heroine doing it alone can often be characterised by loneliness, grief and struggle; and contrary to popular misconception, it is NOT simply having one less pair of hands to help out with the kids. The Muslim heroines I have met that are doing it alone are a hardy bunch. They are, by and large, strong women who have learned to surmount their fears, weaknesses and anxieties, and whose parenting triumphs should be magnified accordingly. They are women of faith who have found even greater faith in God as a result of their situations, who have dug deep and found immense courage and resilience within the chasm. They are women who have had to contend with mental health issues but who continue to do their best, day in day out, for the sake of their children.

For my sisters raising children alone, hang in there: even if it does not like feel like it right now, with difficulty there is ease, and you will find this when you look back on these trying times with hindsight. Whilst bringing up our children alone, we come to realise that we cannot shield them from every hardship and negative emotion, and nor should we. By witnessing our struggles first-hand and seeing us address them with resilience and courage, they in turn will grow up with compassion and perseverance. Even the fact that single-income families may not be able to afford what two-income families can afford, or do as they do, may disappoint children at times, but they will be stronger for it and learn delayed gratification. The silver lining emerges when we see our children mature and appreciate our struggles and the difficult choices we have made, even if it is as late as when they become parents themselves.

For our proverbial village that is supposed to be helping us raise our children, I hope the challenges of mothers doing it alone has struck a chord with fellow parents and highlighted some of their struggles as well as their strengths in overcoming them, but most of all, that support for single mothers in the Muslim community is now long overdue. Every struggling mother needs a well of love to draw from and it is our duty as the village to fill that well. When Prophet Ibrahim (pbuh) had to leave his wife, Hajar and his baby son, Isma'il, in the valley of Makka - which was a city by then, albeit barren - he supplicated for Allah to provide for them, as mentioned in the verse above, but first, to make *people's hearts* incline towards them and look after them. Parents doing it alone, whatever their circumstances, need the support of their community, be it financially, emotionally or at the most basic level, as an extra pair of hands.

وَكُنِ اللّهُمَّ بِعِزَّتِكَ لِيْ فِيْ كُلِّ الْأَحْوَالِ رَؤُوْفًا وَعَلَيَّ فِيْ جَمِيْعِ الْأُمُوْرِ
عَطُوْفًا. إِلٰهِيْ وَرَبِّيْ مَنْ لِيْ غَيْرُكَ أَسْأَلُهُ كَشْفَ ضُرِّيْ وَالنَّظَرَ فِيْ أَمْرِيْ؟

O Allah, I beg you by Your honour, to be compassionate towards me in all circumstances, and to be affectionate towards me in all matters. My God! My Nourisher! Who do I have apart from You whom I can ask to remove my distress and to understand my problems?

(Extract from Du'a Kumayl)

⁂ **Think of the single mothers that you know, or mothers who seem to doing it alone - what could you offer to do to help and support them?**

⁂ **If you are a mother doing it alone, or feeling as if you are doing it alone, even occasionally, how have your challenges made you stronger and strengthened your relationship with God?**

⁂ **What has been the silver lining or the ease hidden within the hardship in your situation?**

22. THERE WILL BE CONSEQUENCES

وَمَا أَصَابَكُم مِّن مُّصِيبَةٍ فَبِمَا كَسَبَتْ أَيْدِيكُمْ وَيَعْفُو عَن كَثِيرٍ

Whatever affliction befalls you is due to what your hands have earned,
and He excuses many [an offense of yours].

(Sūra al-Shūrā 42:30)

'I'm telling you Papa, this is how we're supposed to do it', I insisted to my dad, with my newfound expertise in electric circuits learned that morning in a high school Physics lesson. We had conducted the lightbulb experiment in class, and I was nerdily replicating it at home for my homework. Believing I knew better than my ancient Dad about wires and electricity, and too impatient to listen to his long-winded back-to-basics explanation about live, earth and neutral, I went ahead and plugged the wire into a 13 amp socket to juice a tiny little lightbulb. He watched me, mildly amused, as the fuse blew and I jumped, quite literally frazzled with my hands blackened. Since that day, I have conceded that my dad knows everything about everything, or at least better than I do about a lot of things, and consequently took safety hazards in science experiments a lot more seriously. Had he intervened and pulled the wire out of my hands, or insisted I do it his way, or forced me to listen to him, or not allowed me to continue, the precious lesson would have been lost.

Unfortunately, my dad's wise parenting style was lost on me until much later into my journey as a parent, having spent the first few years very much in helicopter mode (hover over them and help). It wasn't until later that I became more acquainted with the value of allowing children to make mistakes so that they learn from them before becoming adults, and I was amazed to read about it as a technique mentioned by Imam Ali (pbuh), documented in *Nahj al-Balāgha*. He mentions time and again in various sayings and sermons, especially in Letter 31 to his son, about letting experience be your teacher, and about facing the consequences of your actions. He writes, 'A man who masters his experiences will be safe from harm, while a man who is devoid of experiences will be blind to consequences [of actions].'

This is exactly what modern parenting and discipline experts advocate: to allow children to learn from the natural consequences of their mistakes, without added punishment, lectures or interference. So for example, a child who always forgets his homework, PE kit or lunch at home: the authoritarian parent will nag, plead, threaten or lecture; the permissive parent will dutifully remember it for him or even go back home, and come back to drop it off to school; the wise parent, however, will see the forgotten lunch or PE kit as a golden opportunity to let the child learn from the consequences of his own actions. A couple of times without lunch or having to sit out PE, and you can rest assured he won't do that again. No lectures, no punishments, no rewards. And that works all the way up until adulthood. It is not until parents allow children to make mistakes, then learn from them, and let their own experiences be their teacher that the child learns responsibility for his own actions. The more a child is bailed out, rescued and lectured time and time again, the more these precious lessons go to waste.

'What about dangerous things like drugs and other harmful habits?', I hear you ask. 'Surely we can't let our children experience those and learn the hard way!' Imam Ali (pbuh) has an answer for that too. That's when he advocates learning from *others'* experiences. He constantly advises his children and companions to watch people's actions and to learn from them, *'If you find objectionable and loathsome habits in others, abstain from developing those characteristics in yourself. If you are satisfied or feel happy in receiving a certain kind of behaviour from others, you may behave with others in exactly the same way.'* What beautiful advice that is: watch people, watch their interactions, learn from their mistakes and pitfalls so you don't do the same, do unto people the good that you experience from others. The Qur'an too urges at least twelve times for us to 'travel in the land so that you may see the consequences of people's actions' (Sūra al-'Ankabūt 29:20). It teaches us through narrative stories of past people and prophets; 'We narrate to you the best of stories by Our revealing to you this Qur'an.' (Sūra Yusuf 12:1). We're lucky to have TedX talks, Goalcast videos, vlogs, countless parenting and self-help books and documentaries, in addition to travel opportunities whereby we can learn about people's lives beyond our immediate neighbourhood or community, the mistakes they have made, the experiences lived, and lessons understood, and in turn teach our children. We constantly pray for God to protect them from vices and to be fast learners who do not need to learn the hard way as adults.

اَللّٰهُمَّ وَعَلَيَّ تَبِعَاتٌ قَدْ حَفِظْتُهُنَّ وَتَبِعَاتٌ قَدْ نَسِيْتُهُنَّ، وَكُلُّهَا بِعَيْنِكَ الَّتِيْ لَا تَنَامُ وَعِلْمِكَ الَّذِيْ لَا يَنْسَى. فَعَوِّضْ مِنْهَا أَهْلَهَا وَاحْطُطْ عَنِّيْ وِزْرَهَا، وَخَفِّفْ عَنِّيْ ثِقْلَهَا، وَاعْصِمْنِيْ أَنْ أُقَارِفَ مِثْلَهَا.

O Allah upon my head are consequences that I remember and consequences that I have forgotten, but all of them are under Your eye that never sleeps and Your knowledge that never forgets. So compensate those whom they affected, lighten from me their load and protect me from making the same mistake again.

(Extract from Du'a al-Tawba, the Supplication of Repentance by Imam Zayn al-Abidin (pbuh) no. 31 in Sahifa al-Sajjadiyya)

➤ Reflect back on your childhood - was there a significant lesson that you learned from making a mistake?

➤ How do you let your children learn through experiencing the natural consequences of their actions?

23. LETTER THIRTY-ONE: MODERN TEACHING METHODS

وَلَقَدْ ضَرَبْنَا للنَّاسِ فِيْ هَذَا الْقُرْآنِ مِنْ كُلِّ مَثَلٍ لَعَلَّهُمْ يَتَذَكَّرُوْنَ.

And certainly We have coined in this Qur'an every kind of parable for mankind so that they may reflect.

(Sūra al-Zumar 39:27)

"See the ruined cities, the dilapidated palaces, decaying signs and relics of fallen empires of past nations. Then meditate over the activities of those people, what they have all done when they were alive and were in power, what they achieved, from where they started their careers; where, when and how they were brought to an end, where they are now; what have they actually gained out of life and what were their contributions to human welfare,"

Imam Ali (pbuh) writes to his son, encouraging him to travel, to see the world with all its sights and ruins. For a man who lived 1400 years ago, he sure was attuned to modern, inquiry-driven teaching methods.

It is almost with a childlike fascination that he sits and watches the ant, or admires and draws valuable lessons from the peacock, or the solar system. He encouraged his children and people around him to question, saying: *'Knowledge is stored in safes whose key is to question'*. He encouraged them (and us) to ask 'Why?', to reflect and ponder about things, to research and have inquisitive minds.

Another thing I admire about the way he teaches his son is how he illustrates and paints a picture to make it easier to grasp a difficult concept, such as the benefit of charity for example. Sharing and giving things away can be a tricky thing to explain to children who operate on instant gratification: the concept of reaping what you sow here much later on, in a place and time you can't see, smell or touch, or how charity given here will be multiplied manifold over there. But Imam Ali (as) illustrates the lesson beautifully. He says,

'If you find around you such poor, needy and destitute people who are willing to carry your load for you as far as the Day of Judgment then consider this to be a bonus, enlist them and pass your burden on to them; [i.e. Distribute your wealth amongst them and help others to the best of your ability, and be kind and sympathetic to human beings]. *Thus relieve yourself from the heavy responsibility and liability of submitting an account on the Day of Judgement of how you have made use of His Bounties (of health, wealth, power and position), and thus you may arrive at the end of the journey, light and fresh, having enough provision for you there.'*

He goes on to say, *'Have as many porters as possible [i.e. help as many people as you can] so that you when you very badly need them, you do not lack any. Remember that everything that you give out in charity and good deeds are like loans, which will be paid back to you. Therefore, when you are wealthy and powerful, make use of your wealth and power in such a way that you get all that back on the Day of Judgment, when you will be poor and helpless.'*

It is important to explain such concepts to children in a way that they can understand, because although we humans can be altruistic, we mostly give out of pity or feeling sorry for the gaunt, malnourished orphaned baby on the screen, and eventually become hardened to it. We may give to causes only after extensive research into their deservingness. Ultimately, we are self-serving and are motivated most when there's something in it for us. When the human being grasps, however, that the main beneficiary of his charity, who stands to profit the most, *is himself* he will give freely and generously, and that is something that Imam Ali (as) inculcated in his children from young.

There is no principle, moral virtue or valuable lesson that he fails to include in this letter. He teaches him about self-control and anger management, about when to talk and when to remain silent, about bullying and never to tyrannize anybody, and never to let fear of other people prevent you from standing up for someone who is being bullied, about when to assert yourself and have self-esteem and when to display humility.

He teaches him the importance of being surrounded by good people, saying: *'Before ascertaining the conditions of a route, find out what kinds of people will accompany you on the journey. Instead of enquiring about the condition of the home in which you are going to stay, first of all try to find out what kind of people your neighbours are.'* He is so specific in his advice, listing and making clear to him exactly what kind of friends to choose, and what kind of people to avoid becoming too close to. These are all valuable parenting lessons, that both seasoned and new parents alike can learn from in Imam's advice to his son.

Letter 31 of *Nahjul Balagha* is a condensed course in parenting using true, divine morals and virtues, and as we learn from our spiritual father's teachings, confident that unlike self-professed parenting experts out there, he really knew what he was doing, so do we implore Allah to grant us all, the *tawfiq* and strength to be able to emulate these virtues ourselves first, and then be exemplary parents and be able to pass them on to our children, through His Grace, inshallah.

وَاجْعَلْهُمْ أَبْرَارًا أَتْقِيَاءَ بُصَرَاءَ سَامِعِيْنَ مُطِيْعِيْنَ لَكَ وَلِأَوْلِيَاءِكَ مُحِبِّيْنَ مُنَاصِحِيْنَ وَلِجَمِيْعِ أَعْدَائِكَ مُعَانِدِيْنَ وَمُبْغِضِيْنَ... وَأَعِنِّيْ عَلَى تَرْبِيَتِهِمْ وَتَأْدِيْبِهِمْ وَبَرِّهِمْ...

*Make them (my children) pious, God-conscious, insightful, good
listeners and obedient towards You, loving and well-disposed towards
Your friends, and resistant and averse to Your enemies. And help me
in their upbringing and education, and to be devoted to them.*

(Extract from Du'a' 25 of Sahifa al-Sajjadiyya: Imam Zayn al-Abidin's
Supplication for His Children)

〜 **Why not open Letter 31 today: what nuggets of wisdom can
you find in it that you could apply to your life?**

〜 **How has Imam Ali (pbuh)'s picture of needy people
receiving our charity as porters changed your view of giving
in charity?**

24. YOU'VE BROKEN MY TRUST

إِنَّا عَرَضْنَا الْأَمَانَةَ عَلَى السَّمَاوَاتِ وَالْأَرْضِ وَالْجِبَالِ فَأَبَيْنَ أَنْ يَحْمِلْنَهَا وَأَشْفَقْنَ مِنْهَا وَحَمَلَهَا الْإِنْسَانُ إِنَّهُ كَانَ ظَلُومًا جَهُولًا.

We did indeed offer the trust to the heavens, the earth and the mountains, but they refused to undertake it, being afraid thereof; but man undertook it - he was indeed unjust and foolish.

(Sūra al-Aḥzāb 33:72)

One of the most painful emotions that parents can experience is a sense of betrayal and bitter disappointment when our trust in our beloved, angelic children has been broken by them. Whether the breach takes the form of a lie, a lost valuable item, a blatant misdemeanour or even more serious things done behind our backs, the pain can cripple us. Some of us take it very personally when our children break our trust, even though we may have been guilty of the same with our own parents in our youth or even still as adults. We find it very difficult to trust them again, guarding our hearts from being hurt, as we would if fellow adults had broken our trust. But whilst a breach in trust can be paralysing for us as well as our children, we cannot be naïve in thinking that our children will forever remain innocent and not toe - or even overstep - the line.

I will never forget the very first time I caught one of my children lying and doing something behind my back. And I am sure he/she won't either, because of how devastated I was and how dramatic my reaction! I lectured and preached, scowled and frowned, showed my utter disappointment and even disgust at the behaviour, and of course, grounded them. I made them apologise, make amends and promise never to do it again. And guess what? In spite of all that, they did it again. And again after that. Because that is human nature if left untrained. God Himself, in the verse above, describes the human being as unjust and foolish with His trust that he so hastily took on, which the heavens, earth and mountains were too cautious to bear.

Trust, like all other noble virtues such as honesty, courage, generosity and sincerity, requires training and education. To expect our children to be automatically trustworthy is a little naïve if we have not yet trained them properly. Training is not done through lectures and 'telling them' but through giving them lots of opportunities to practice.

The first step is to believe them when they say that they will not do it again. It is all too tempting to bring up the past periodically and well-meaningly remind them of what *not* to do again and again. Instead we must genuinely show them that trust *can* be rebuilt and that we have faith that they will be able to rebuild it, and most of all that *we* are there to help them rebuild it.

Parents, once bitten, are twice shy when it comes to loosening the grip on their children when trust has been breached. It makes sense that if they are not going to take a responsibility or privilege seriously, then they should not be given it. Even Prophet Yaʿqub (pbuh) after his sons had so grossly betrayed his trust and had supposedly 'lost' Yusuf - the apple of his eye - to a hungry wolf, found it very difficult to trust them again; even years down the line as adults, when they asked to take Binyamin, his youngest son, to Egypt with them. He said, 'Shall I trust you with him, except as I trusted you with his brother before?' (Sūra Yusuf 12:64). Knowing the kind of act they had been capable of, he naturally found it difficult to trust them again, even as grown men. Regardless, he then went on to place his own trust in God, invoked Him as the best Keeper, and entrusted Binyamin to them.

Counter-intuitively then, it is exactly that which we too must do, especially when our children are still young and mouldable. We need to express more faith in them, and give them small tasks to accomplish, trust them with things whereby we can 'catch' them fulfilling that trust or responsibility. We train them by giving them more and more opportunities to first make amends, then mend the trust. To prove and affirm to themselves that they are indeed trustworthy. It is up to us to help our children succeed by catching them doing good things and fulfilling trusts many many times, and drawing their attention to how good they are at putting things back in their rightful place, returning library books, looking after other people's belongings, telling the truth and keeping their word, rather than only catching them breaking our trust and reminding them of their past mistakes repeatedly.

Keeping trusts and promises are cornerstones of Islamic ethics and essential qualities that we need to have mastered as responsible adults. As parents, we absolutely cannot afford to break our promises to our children, or lie to them about anything, as it sets the tone for them to resort to taking our word lightly, as well as their own. Realistically though, the breaking of trust from our young children is something that we, as parents, must anticipate and prepare for, just as the breaking of dishes or vases, because unfortunately as humans, we are fallible and foolish. Do we ourselves not break our covenants with God, and go back on our word time and time again? And He continues to give us so many chances to prove ourselves to him. Our children will break our trust from time to time, but thankfully, unlike glasses and vases that shatter into pieces and can't be restored, our trust can be repaired (to a certain extent). We must endeavour to mend it together by giving them opportunities to do so, just as God makes allowances for us. And whilst it is true that trust must be 'earned', when it comes to children, trustworthiness must first be 'learned'.

رَبَّنَا لاَ تُؤَاخِذْنَا إِن نَّسِينَا أَوْ أَخْطَأْنَا رَبَّنَا وَلاَ تَحْمِلْ عَلَيْنَا إِصْرًا كَمَا حَمَلْتَهُ عَلَى الَّذِينَ مِن قَبْلِنَا رَبَّنَا وَلاَ تُحَمِّلْنَا مَا لاَ طَاقَةَ لَنَا بِهِ وَاعْفُ عَنَّا وَاغْفِرْ لَنَا وَارْحَمْنَا أَنتَ مَوْلاَنَا فَانصُرْنَا عَلَى الْقَوْمِ الْكَافِرِينَ.

...O our Lord, do not hold us responsible if we forget or make mistake. O our lord, do not lay on us a burden such as you laid on those before us. O our Lord, do not impose upon us that which we have not the strength (to bear). Pardon us, and forgive us, and have mercy on us. You are our lord-master, so help us against the unbelieving people.

(Sūra al-Baqara 2:286)

》﹏ **How did you learn lessons in trustworthiness during your own childhood?**

》﹏ **If this is something that you find challenging with your children, what kind of opportunities to 'learn' trust can you implement in your household today?**

_____

_____

_____

_____

_____

25. LOOK AT ME WHEN I SPEAK TO YOU

وَفِي الْأَرْضِ آيَاتٌ لِلْمُوْقِنِيْنَ. وَفِيْ أَنْفُسِكُمْ ۚ أَفَلَا تُبْصِرُوْنَ.

And in the earth there are signs for those who have conviction, and in your own souls too; will you then not perceive?

(Sūra al-Dhāriyāt 51:20-21)

I often find myself saying to my children 'Look at me when I speak to you', even though I know that they can hear me just fine. I know that they are listening from their grunts or mumbles, and yet it makes such a difference to me when they look at me, and we make eye contact and actually see each other. In other cultures, it is considered disrespectful to look directly at a parent when they are addressing you, looking down instead. To me, however, it was important that they see the look on my own face, and my expression.

Ironically, this time I was not the one saying these words but my 7-year old daughter, trying to get my attention as she babbled away about her friend's cartwheels at school, and I was guilty as charged: merely mumbling an *uhuh* and *hmmm* now and again without looking up at her. That is actually one of the first principles of active listening - to look at the person who is speaking and to make eye-contact. When my children were little, I would even resort to gently lifting their chins up to look at me so they could see my face when I was trying to communicate something that they found difficult to hear. Somehow, people do not feel heard when we do not look at them, feeling ignored and unimportant. Whilst we can hear just fine with our ears, listening is done with both the eyes and ears. Sight and hearing are so closely linked together that even Allah often juxtaposes His two Names, *al-Samī'* (The all-Hearing) and *al-Baṣīr* (The all-Seeing) next to each other.

In His Book of guidance to us, He constantly urges us to 'look up' when He's speaking to us and communicating with us. He asks to 'observe', to 'look around', 'to look up' at the sky, 'to see', 'to perceive', to 'open our eyes', and asks: 'Do you not see?' more than 250 times in the Qur'an. He asks us repeatedly, '*Are the blind and the seeing the same?*' (Sūra al-An'ām 6:50) God does not want to have to lead us by having to pull our chins up as we stare blankly at the pages of His guidance, and at the signs that He has scattered all around our line of vision and inside our own souls, so He asks us rhetorically, '*Do you not then perceive?*' He continually draws our attention through imagery of deaf, mute and blind people being like cattle in Sūra al-Baqara, or tunnel-visioned people in Sūra Yāsīn who only see what is directly in front of them and do not heed His message. God wants us to listen to Him with our eyes, just as we want our children to listen to us with their eyes.

Listening with the eyes starts very young, and God has given parents a very powerful tool to help guide their children aright when they are misbehaving, without having to say a word. It's called 'The Look'. Every parent knows about The Look. My mother used to use it in the mosque to get us to sit up straight and not slouch. Others use it to cast firm warnings to their children when they speak out of turn and are about to do or say something to show them up. Others overuse The Look and are in a perpetual state of 'Look-giving'. Then there are those who have not yet mastered the art of The Look, unable to pull it off without a smirk or giggle - they have to resort to asking grandparents, aunties and uncles to give their unruly children a stern Look. The Look worked beautifully before screens took over our world. Now, unfortunately, a parent can be throwing The Look with all his might, one eyebrow arched and eyes squinting, charged with radioactive fury, but the unsuspecting child is too fixated on his colourful screen to even glance up and bat an eyelid at his parent's magic weapon.

Looking up and really listening, really perceiving, is a skill that we need to remind ourselves to do, and to train our young ones to do, both for the sake of our communication in the home, as well as for us to take in God's messages and His communication to us. We can only be receptive when we look up and take notice of what is being said. We must encourage as much time as possible away from screens, both ourselves and our children, especially on car journeys. Whilst it is tempting to hand them an iPad and not hear a peep out of them, there is so much to see, so much to look at and draw lesson from in nature outdoors. Make a game out of it: I Spy works beautifully as does Pictures in the Clouds, What Am I, and many other games that require us to look around, to ask questions, to read facial expressions, and to sharpen our observation skills.

We, of course, must model that behaviour first with our own screens, and especially when our children are trying to tell us something - to actually look at their little faces, make eye contact, and really listen with our eyes. That's the only way that they will learn to listen to us and others with their eyes. And we must listen to all of it, even the small stuff: the seemingly insignificant details about their day, their friends, their games and their funny ideas, so that when it comes to the big, important issues later on, they will continue coming to talk to us, because for children, what we consider small stuff is already big and important to them.

Allah often addresses 'the people of insight' (ulū'l-abṣar) in the Qur'an, and tells them that He has placed in various things signs for them to ponder over. Insight is born out of sharp eyesight, not the 20-20 vision kind, but rather an ability to draw lessons, to read expressions and to perceive. The people of insight are those who understand the ways of the unseen without needing to 'see' everything, as Imam Ali said he did. *'Would I worship a God I cannot see?'* he stated. And conversely, about the people who reject God's signs and refuse to look up and ponder, shutting the eyes of their heart tightly and blocking out the light, God says, 'Allah won't even look at them or speak to them on the Day of Judgment.'(Sūra Āl 'Imran 3:77). I cannot imagine a more disheartening feeling than my Creator not even giving me a second glance when I address Him!

اللّهمَّ اجْعلْ النُّوْرَ فِيْ بَصَرِيْ وَالْبَصِيْرَةَ فِيْ دِيْنِيْ وَالْيَقِيْنَ فِيْ قَلْبِيْ
وَالإِخْلاَصَ فِيْ عَمَلِيْ وَالسَّلاَمَةَ فِيْ نَفْسِيْ وَالسَّعَةَ فِيْ رِزْقِيْ والشُّكْرَ لَكَ
أَبَدًا مَا أَبْقَيْتَنِيْ.

O God, place for me light in my eyesight, insight in my religion, conviction in my heart, sincerity in my actions, safety in my soul, ampleness in my provision, and gratitude to You as long as You keep me alive.

(Du'a taught by the Prophet (pbuh) and recommended
to supplicate after *fajr* prayers)

꙳ **When are some of the times that you do not feel listened to?**

꙳ **What are some of the ways you could encourage listening with eyes in your household?**

26. THE WIND AND THE SUN

فَبِمَا رَحْمَةٍ مِنَ اللهِ لِنْتَ لَهُمْ وَلَوْ كُنْتَ فَظًّا غَلِيظًا
لَانْفَضُّوا مِنْ حَوْلِكَ...

...Had you been rough and hard-hearted, they would certainly have scattered from around you...

(Sūra Āl 'Imrān 3:159)

The North Wind and the Sun were disputing which was the stronger, when a traveller came along wrapped in a warm cloak. They agreed that the one who first succeeded in making the traveller take his cloak off should be considered stronger than the other. Then the North Wind blew as hard as he could, but the more he blew the more closely did the traveller fold his cloak around him; and at last the North Wind gave up the attempt. Then the Sun shined out warmly, and immediately the traveller took off his cloak. And so the North Wind was obliged to confess that the Sun was the stronger of the two -

Aesop's Fables.

I often feel like I'm the North Wind when I'm trying to persuade my children to do something - to put on their coats because it's cold outside, to sit down and revise for their exams, to put down their phones, to finish their dinner, to buckle down to studies, to clean their rooms, the list is endless! It often feels like a battle where I try to convince them using my reasoning, logicising, persuading, reminding them of the rules, and even pleading to get them to see things from my point of view. Somehow, the North Wind approach of enforcing just does not work. It is only much later, with hindsight, that it occurs to me that I could have done it a different way - the Sun way, and maybe they would have co-operated. In the moment though, it hardly ever dawns on me to do so.

Recently, however, I got one such opportunity which, I am sure, will resonate with you. A few years ago, my son and I were at an informal event at the high school where he had started attending a few months prior. Parents were invited to visit classrooms, and mingle with their children's teachers. As we made our way around some of the classrooms, one of his subject teachers, instead of giving us a tour of the classroom and explaining the syllabus as he was supposed to do, took the opportunity to have a little 'parent-teacher-consultation' style chat with me about my son's lack of progress, lack of homework and that he did not find him competent at the subject. As my son stood, visibly embarrassed and angry, I was fuming inside, annoyed at the teacher for having spoken out of turn, but especially frustrated with my son's nonchalance with his studies. How could I make him understand that such slackness was intolerable? How could he be so careless just a few months into a new school? I could feel a really good lecture bubbling up inside me, with bullet points and everything, ready to burst forth at the first opportunity alone in a quiet corridor. As we continued with the rest of the evening, my son kept himself guarded, and I could tell he anticipated the unleashing of my wrath at any moment. The quiet corridor and, with it, the chance to tell him off, did not come until we were sat back in the car on the way home, by which my anger had simmered down (thank God!).

I looked at him, gave him a hug said, 'I was really annoyed at the way that teacher spoke about you right in front of you. Regardless of how badly you may be doing, he had no right humiliating you like that. And his timing was all wrong.' My son was not expecting that. He confessed that he had not been doing his best, and that his teacher had not been entirely wrong, and that he was determined to try harder and prove to him that he was perfectly capable of pulling his socks up and doing well at that subject. I was dumbstruck: he himself had come out with the common sense that I had hoped a good telling-off would knock into him, but it was a thousand times more effective than if it had come out of my mouth. His words and change in attitude were literally music to my ears, which I was convinced would not have been the case if my approach had been North Wind-like. He would have become defensive, and angrier, wrapping his cloak of 'rightness' even tighter around himself. By warmly showing him that I was his ally and that I was on his side, and cared about his feelings, it gave him the space to come to his own realization, without any force, persuasion or reasoning on my part. The Sun had won the day! If only all my days and interactions with my children were as sunny.

Sunny and warm was exactly how our beloved Prophet (pbuh)'s demeanour and approach with people was. He was known to be gentle and kind with them, and most people were initially drawn to Islam, not as a result of its logical teachings, but due to his magnetic and warm personality. The above verse addresses him, saying, that if he had been harsh or hard-hearted with people, they would definitely have left him, and that it was by God's mercy that he was so gentle and lenient with them. As a role model for us, his example teaches us that gentleness and warmth have a much more lasting and better effect on people, and this works for our children too. Of course, our lectures, tellings-off and controlling ways of persuasion stem from our looking out for their best interests. Of course, we only do it for their own good - and the lectures do have their place sometimes. But mostly, the lesson is lost in the words that we harshly blow out of our mouths like the North Wind, and it takes warm, empathetic actions showing them that we care for them and are truly on their side to subtly tease out what they already know deep down to be good for them. It's no wonder that Imam Sadiq (pbuh) said, '*The one who is lenient and gentle in his affairs will obtain whatever he wants from people.*'

اَللّٰهُمَّ صَلِّ عَلَى مُحَمَّدٍ وَآلِهِ وَحَلِّنِي بِحِلْيَةِ الصَّالِحِينَ وَأَلْبِسْنِي زِينَةَ الْمُتَّقِينَ فِي بَسْطِ الْعَدْلِ، وَكَظْمِ الْغَيْظِ، وَإِطْفَاءِ النَّائِرَةِ، وَضَمِّ أَهْلِ الْفُرْقَةِ، وَإِصْلَاحِ ذَاتِ الْبَيْنِ، وَإِفْشَاءِ الْعَارِفَةِ، وَسَتْرِ الْعَائِبَةِ، وَلِينِ الْعَرِيكَةِ, وَخَفْضِ الْجَنَاحِ، وَحُسْنِ السِّيرَةِ، وَسُكُونِ الرِّيحِ ...

O God, bless Muhammad and his Household, adorn me with the adornment of the righteous and clothe me in the ornaments of the God-conscious through spreading justice, restraining rage, quenching the flame of resentment, bringing together people who are separated, correcting discord, spreading good conduct, covering faults, mildness of temper, humbleness, beautiful conduct, gravity of bearing...

(Extract from Imam Zayn al-Abidin (pbuh)'s Du'a Makārim al-Akhlāq: his Supplication for Noble Moral Traits no.20 in Sahifa al-Sajjadiyya)

⋙ **What are some of the challenges that drive you into North-Wind-mode with your children?**

⋙ **How could you creatively introduce warmth and gentleness into some of the daily tasks in which you face resistance from your children?**

27. MORE THAN 'JUST A MUM'

إِنَّمَا أَمْوَالُكُمْ وَأَوْلَادُكُمْ فِتْنَةٌ وَاللهُ عِنْدَهُ أَجْرٌ عَظِيمٌ. فَاتَّقُوا اللهَ مَا
اسْتَطَعْتُمْ وَاسْمَعُوا وَأَطِيْعُوا وَأَنْفِقُوا خَيْرًا لِأَنْفُسِكُمْ ۚ وَمَنْ يُوْقَ
شُحَّ نَفْسِهِ فَأُولَئِكَ هُمُ الْمُفْلِحُوْنَ.

*Your possessions and your children are only a trial, and Allah it is
with Whom there is a great reward. Therefore, be as God-conscious
as you can, hear, obey, and spend in charity for the good of your own
souls; and whoever is saved from the avarice of his own soul, these are
indeed the successful.*

(Sūra al-Taghābun 64:15-16)

When children come along, our whole world begins to revolve
around them, which admittedly is quite necessary in the beginning
considering we are their world. They need us to provide for them
and to give them our time, love, affection and support. They are fully
dependant on us. Whilst we are necessarily the centre of their lives,
is it necessary or even healthy for them to be the centre of ours to the
extent where we begin to lose ourselves in our children? Not only
does our daily routine revolve around them, but also our thoughts,
dreams and sense of identity.

People base their sense of worth, lives, callings and joy in all
sorts of things. Some may find their identity in what they do as a
profession, or in their achievements and successes; others base it on
their possessions, assets or net worth. What is it that defines who
we really are? Does our identity lie in our parenthood? Who were
we before we had children who took over our lives? Parenthood is a
sacred and noble calling, but it cannot be the primary source of our

identity - we are more than just parents. The *ayah* above reminds us that our possessions and children are only a trial and a means on our individual paths as souls towards God. The commandment is not to get sucked in to making them the centre of our worlds, but instead to be as God-conscious as possible, to be active in acts of obedience and charity, and to find our higher calling. Giving of ourselves in charity is highlighted as especially good for our souls' wellbeing.

I have struggled many times, and sometimes still do, to remind myself of this fact: that whilst motherhood is a calling, it is not my only calling. Sometimes it can even stand in the way of my greater calling on this earth, when I make it the be-all and end-all of my purpose on this earth. We have dreams and desires burning inside us for a reason, and when we hold off on them for too long, beyond our children's physical dependence on us, those dreams and visions of doing greater good in the world fade away into fantasy.

Your dreams might include starting your own business, writing a book, taking up a fundraising project, revisiting an old hobby, discovering new ones, or volunteering in a community organisation. God has gifted us with the dreams and has wired us with our individual, special talents to make those a reality, and make a difference in the lives of others. Being a mum does not mean that we cannot pursue God's calling to serve Him in other ways, and in fact, being a mum is a stepping stone towards serving others when our skills of empathy, patience and listening get sharpened day by day. Sure, your children may be very young right now, where your sole purpose may indeed be raising them, where it may be physically impossible to leave them for any length of time, and nor should you. Your role at the moment is paramount and is exactly where you need to be. Mothering is your current career – a very noble one at that - and you should treat it as such, putting your very best into it, researching into the best strategies and tools to use, and setting worthy goals within it, for there is much work to be done here.

I remember as a young mother of three children under six, feeling like my identity was just 'mummy'. There was so much I wanted to do but couldn't: joining the gym, teaching at the Sunday School, undertaking charity projects, going back to university to pursue a postgrad, taking my career further. I remember voicing my exasperations to an older auntie who used to teach my children how to read the Qur'an. She lovingly and wisely said to me, 'But it's not your time yet, my dear. Your time will come. But not now. For now, keep dreaming and planning.' Those words of hers have stayed with me.

Our current and very essential roles, wherever we are in our mothering journey, must not stop us from dreaming, from having a vision, from planning ahead and praying hard for God to show us our purpose on this earth. It's okay to desire adult conversation and loftier pursuits than just feeding, burping and school-running, for parenthood is a role like all other roles we take on, albeit a very long one. We are primarily souls in our own right, before any of our roles and beyond them, and we are fortunate to be living in a world where opportunities abound, where women are appreciated for skills beyond child-rearing and homemaking, which our grandmothers were limited to.

When we became parents, we did not un-become everything we were before. Everything we have been is everything that got us to this path. While parenting our little ones, we can be committed to developing ourselves through them, daring to explore all the different sides of who we are. We are multifaceted and we have so much more to give than meets the eye. Let's not leave our 'selves' behind. We need to allow ourselves opportunities to thrive, not just survive.

اللّٰهُمَّ صَلِّ عَلَى مُحَمَّدٍ وَّآلِه وَاكْفِنِيْ مَا يَشْغَلُنِيْ الْاِهْتِمَامُ به وَاسْتَعْمِلْنِيْ بِمَا تسْأَلُنِيْ غَدًا عَنْهُ، وَاسْتَفْرِغْ أَيَّامِيْ فِيْمَا خَلَقْتَنِيْ لَهُ، وَأَغْنِنِيْ وَأَوْسِعْ عَلَيَّ فِيْ رِزْقِكَ... وَأَجْرِ لِلنَّاسِ عَلَى يَدِيَ الْخَيْرَ...

O God, bless Muhammad and His household, and spare me the concerns that distract me, employ me in that which You will ask me about tomorrow, and let me pass my days for that which You have created me. Free me from need and expand Your provision toward me... Let good flow out from my hands towards people...

(Extract from Imam Zayn al-Abidin (pbuh)'s Du'a Makārim al-Akhlāq: his Supplication for Noble Moral Traits no. 20 in Sahifa al-Sajjadiyya)

➤ Do you ever feel like there are dreams and desires that God has placed in your heart to pursue? What are they?

➤ What are the biggest obstacles standing in the way of pursuing your calling?

➤ Take time to consider what your deepest values and strengths are and how your identity is crafted beyond your role as a mother.

28. I DID NOT SIGN UP FOR THIS

وَكَذَٰلِكَ مَكَّنَّا لِيُوسُفَ فِي الْأَرْضِ يَتَبَوَّأُ مِنْهَا حَيْثُ يَشَاءُ ۚ نُصِيبُ
بِرَحْمَتِنَا مَن نَّشَاءُ ۖ وَلَا نُضِيعُ أَجْرَ الْمُحْسِنِينَ.

And thus did we give Yusuf power in the land - he had mastery in it
wherever he liked. We send down Our mercy on whom We please,
and We do not waste the reward of those who do good.

(Sūra Yusuf 12:56)

Sitting with a few friends in a café at the end of December 2018, grabbing a coffee and chat together before our children broke up from school for the holidays, we reviewed the year on its way out and each took stock of our gains and losses, and how it had been for us. The session turned out to be one big whingeing session - interspersed with customary *Alhamdulillahs* here and there (of course) - as all four of us felt that the year had been quite unfair, and that we were each stuck in a rut with little control over our lives. Collectively, we had faced financial loss, health issues, problems with our teens, marital problems, car accidents and a whole host of other things that had not lived up to our expectations and high hopes at the start of the year. All of us felt that we had not signed up to these difficulties, in spite of being faithful, practicing, Muslim women, and frankly we felt stuck as to how to approach 2019 differently and somehow have it flow in our favour.

It is so easy to feel stuck or disheartened when we have a bad day, bad week, bad month and a bad year, and to feel a lack of control or ownership over our lives, especially for those control-freaks like me, who abhor change and unpredictability. We wanted to own 2019 but couldn't think how! When I read the verses above, about how Allah empowered Prophet Yusuf (pbuh) and gave him mastery and control over Egypt's storehouses after having been a powerless child, kidnapped and trafficked into slavery, it filled me with awe and hope. Yusuf (pbuh) did not merely have a bad year, by our standards; he had a bad life, in that he had no control whatsoever in most of the things that happened to him growing up. He certainly had not signed up for his jealous brothers' plot to sell him into slavery, nor to be taken to a foreign land away from his loving parents, nor to be falsely accused of seducing his master's wife and thrown in jail. In all of this he was powerless, and his unjust circumstances could have easily had him complaining: 'God, I didn't sign up for this.' or 'What have I done to deserve this?' He could have retaliated against those who caused his turmoil. But he didn't.

When we read between the lines in the Qur'an, its verses indicate to us that Prophet Yusuf (pbuh) did not remain victim to whatever fate's hand dealt him. He took ownership of his situation whenever and wherever possible, and maintained his dignity, his principles and his moral compass at all cost. When faced with the plot of the lustful women of the city, he beseeched God that he would prefer life in prison over succumbing to their suggestions, even when he had no autonomy or hope of freedom as a slave. He expressed to God that being stuck in sin would be far worse an enslavement than being stuck in a prison cell. He maintained his innocence, even to people who ignored him. When he was finally released from prison, after interpreting the king's dreams and advising him with the correct course of action, he first took ownership of his situation and took the opportunity to change his destiny by saying to the king, *'Place me in charge of the treasuries of the land; surely I am a good keeper and knowledgeable.'* (Sūra Yusuf 12:55). He could have easily accepted his lot in life as a falsely imprisoned slave with no rights or advocates, but he knew his own strengths, and trusted that God helps those who help themselves and are fully committed to goodness. He fearlessly and proactively put himself forward for the lofty task of chief-treasurer.

God, in turn, says, '*And thus did we give Yusuf power in the land - he had mastery in it wherever he liked. We send down Our mercy on whom We please, and We do not waste the reward of those who do good.*' (Sūra Yusuf 12:56) His positive attitude and ownership over his talents and skills, using them for good, and refusal to succumb to victimhood paid off, and he did not remain at the mercy of his circumstances.

Towards the end of the story, we get a glimpse of how he treated his brothers when the tables were turned and he had the upper hand. From having been a slave of men and circumstances, he was now a powerful governor, in charge of the granary. And his brothers came from their famine-ridden land to humbly barter grain from him. After finally realising his true identity, they feared he would retaliate for the cruel way in which they had treated him, but instead, ever wise and discerning, he says, 'There shall be no reproof against you on this day; may God forgive you, and He is the most merciful of the merciful.' (Sūra Yusuf 12:92)

In the story of Prophet Yusuf, we see a man who - although stuck smack bang in the middle of a heap of setbacks and difficult situations that he never signed up for - refused to let life's hard knocks knock him off course and prevent him from a life that pleased God. Whether a slave or a king, his moral compass never changed and nor his proactive attitude towards life. He believed in a God that grants kingdom to those who take ownership of their situation, in a God who orchestrates everything for good and never wastes the reward of those who do good, for in His Hands is only good.

أَللهُمَّ مَالِكَ الْمُلْكِ تُؤْتِي الْمُلْكَ مَن تَشَاءُ وَتَنزِعُ الْمُلْكَ مِمَّن تَشَاءُ
وَتُعِزُّ مَن تَشَاءُ وَتُذِلُّ مَن تَشَاءُ ۖ بِيَدِكَ الْخَيْرُ ۖ
إِنَّكَ عَلَىٰ كُلِّ شَيْءٍ قَدِيرٌ.

*O Allah, Master of all sovereignty! You give sovereignty to whomever
You wish, and strip of sovereignty whomever You wish; You make
mighty whomever You wish, and You degrade whomever You wish; all
goodness is in Your hand. Indeed, You have power over all things.*

(Sūra Āl ʿImrān 3:26 - recommended to recite after *fajr*)

〽 **What aspect of your life has tempted you to protest, 'But I
didn't sign up for this!'?**

〽 **How can Prophet Yusuf 's example help you to take
ownership of your circumstances?**

_____

_____

_____

_____

_____

_____

29. TEACHING REPENTANCE

إِلَّا مَنْ تَابَ وَآمَنَ وَعَمِلَ عَمَلًا صَالِحًا فَأُولَئِكَ يُبَدِّلُ اللهُ سَيِّئَاتِهِمْ حَسَنَاتٍ ۚ وَكَانَ اللهُ غَفُورًا رَحِيْمًا.

...except he who repents and believes and does a good deed; so these are the ones whose evil deeds Allah transforms to good ones; and Allah is Forgiving, Merciful.

(Sūra al-Furqān 25:70)

'You need to apologise to your sister!' I insisted to my eldest after his latest round of teasing and winding up had left her upset while we were on a long car ride back home. He sniggered and said, quite sarcastically, 'Sorrrraaay!' That, of course, set me off on a rant, 'That's not an apology. Say it like you mean it. And be nice to her - when you upset someone, saying sorry doesn't do much until you actually make amends for your misbehaviour.' He stated plainly that in that case he would do it when he was good and ready to do something nice for her, and when he actually felt like apologising, not just because I said so. Fair point, I guess, since the very first criteria for repentance is sincerity. At the time though I didn't see it his way. I heard backchat, and snapped. Clearly even more crabby and impatient than my three bickering children, I had a full-on meltdown! All of the emotion boiled over inside of me, and I raised my voice and yelled, letting my anger at his 'defiance' get the better of me. For a good minute or two, I gave all three of them an earful.

In the process of being a peace-maker, I had failed miserably. Ironically, I was bellowing at them not to bicker, shouting at them to be nice to each other, and yelling at them for not apologising on my terms. Evidently, I needed a dose of my own advice first! And so I had to eat my own words, calm down and apologise to them, 'I'm sorry guys, please forgive me.' There in the car, I had to remind the children that their mother wasn't perfect and needed to apologise for losing her cool. The content of my lecture may have been correct, but the sharp way in which I delivered it was wounding.

This wasn't the kind of teaching moment I would prefer! I'd much rather tell a story, share an anecdote about why forgiveness is necessary, or give them examples about how God transforms bad deeds into good ones when we do good to those we have wronged. Instead, I had to *be* the example. But there was something very powerful in that exchange where I was forced to model the steps to repentance that I had been telling them: sincerely apologising to them, describing exactly what I was saying sorry for, what I could have done instead, and actually making amends to them.

My meltdown in the car was certainly not the first time I lost my cool, and it definitely was not the last. As parents, we often fall short and so do our tempers. Exhaustion and stress can leave us vulnerable to mistakes instead of always being a shining example for our kids, and at times this is inevitable as we are not perfect. In moments like those, it is important not to get carried away in the emotion, and to acknowledge our mistakes when we make them, even to our children, for God uses precisely those moments of shortcoming for good.

Our missteps can be great opportunities for us to model to them how we lean into God, how to feel remorse, what is acceptable behaviour and what is not, even from adults. As the verse above states, God has the power to transform misdeeds into good ones, and our stumbles into great teaching moments for us as well as our children when we repent. As long as they do not happen too frequently, they get to see not only our mistakes but also repentance in action, and God's favour upon us all.

رَبَّنَا اغْفِرْ لَنَا ذُنُوْبَنَا وَإِسْرَافَنَا فِيْ أَمْرِنَا وَثَبِّتْ أَقْدَامَنَا وَانْصُرْنَا عَلَى الْقَوْمِ الْكَافِرِيْنَ.

Our Lord! Forgive us our sins and our excesses in our affairs, and make our feet steady, and help us against the faithless lot.

(Sūra Āl ʿImrān 3:147)

〰️ **When are you most vulnerable to having a meltdown?**

〰️ **It's easy to just demand for a conflict to be over, and peace and quiet to return. What could you do to truly teach forgiveness in your household rather than simply end the conflicts?**

_____

_____

_____

_____

_____

_____

30. FRIEND OR FRENEMY?

إِنَّ الشَّيْطَانَ لَكُمْ عَدُوٌّ فَاتَّخِذُوهُ عَدُوًّا

Surely Satan is a manifest enemy to you, so treat him as an enemy.

(Sūra al-Fāṭir 35:6)

I love to learn new words, and have a screensaver on my laptop that teaches me a new word a day from the dictionary. I find it quite intriguing how new words are actually created and then added into the English language and to dictionaries through common usage. Merriam-Webster added more than 1000 new words to its guide in 2018, giving the thumbs-up to lots of texting and internet slang like 'TL DR' (too long, didn't read) and 'bingeable', as well as new abbreviations for favourite foods like 'zoodles', 'avo' and 'guac'. One such word I came across a couple of years ago was *frenemy*, which is defined as: one who pretends to be a friend but is actually an enemy.

Whilst frenemies have always existed, even at the time of the Prophets and the Imams (pbut), this era of social-networking sites has given particular rise to the number of frenemies lurking in the shadows behind screens and keyboards. We hear of schoolgirls accepting someone as a friend on Snapchat or Insta, not because they really like her and want to be her friend, but to spy on her and keep up with what's happening in her life, stalking, trolling and cyber-bullying. Even grown women befriend people on Facebook just to poke their noses around what people are doing, where they go on holiday and what they're eating! In reality, they can't stand some of these 'friends' so the backbiting and tongue-wagging continue even as their profile photos smile sweetly at each other: fake, false...frenemies.

It's important to be aware of frenemies in our own lives and to teach our children about the qualities of good friends, and how to tell them apart from frenemies.

Our Imams consciously warned their true companions about hypocritical people and a class of sycophants called *ghulāt* who would raise the Imams above their God-given status, flattering them, attributing superpowers to them and then betraying their secrets. Frenemies have a lot in common with the greatest frenemy of them all - the arch-deceiver. God describes his plots in a lot of detail in the Qur'an, how he tricks and traps, leaving us regretting our choices the way he did to Adam and Hawwa (Sūra al-A'rāf 7:27). His ways sparkle, glitter and entice, making false promises of fantastical illusions, which end up being mere shadows (Sūra Ṭāhā 20:120). He photoshops reality and entices us with ever-so-subtle subliminal messages. He makes our deeds fair-seeming to us (Sūra al-'Ankabūt 29:38), and promises to be a sincere adviser (Sūra al-A'rāf 7:21) like a wolf in sheep's clothing, who comes to steal, kill and sow enmity between people. He gradually baits us and reels us in when we least expect it (Sūra al-A'rāf 7:22), using our good deeds to sow seeds of pride and self-admiration, dissipating them like vinegar on honey. He whispers irrational fears of poverty, enticing us to fraud and indecency (Sūra al-Baqara 2:268), fanning the embers of anxiety that turn into great flames of fear and mistrust in God's provision. He double-crosses us and makes us doubt in our own abilities and our God-given gifts, so we take them to be a curse instead.

And Allah warns us over and over again in the Qur'an about him and tells us not to follow his footsteps. He describes him in the clearest words possible, in black and white: *Surely Shaytan is an enemy to you, so treat him as an enemy*. Do not befriend him, though he poses as a friend, he is the greatest frenemy of them all. In addition, God has also told us that what makes people more susceptible to Shaytan's guiles and insinuations is their unawareness of his ploys, and their heedlessness of God's remembrance. He says, *"Whoever turns himself away from the remembrance of the All-Merciful, We appoint for him a Shaytan, and so he becomes his close friend."* (Sūra al-Zukhruf 43:36). But the opposite is also true, that those who resort to Him, and seek refuge only in Him, He protects from Shaytan and his whisperings.

رَبِّ أَعُوْذُ بِكَ مِنْ هَمَزَاتِ الشَّيَاطِيْنَ وَأَعُوْذُ بِكَ رَبِّ أَنْ يَحْضُرُوْنَ.

"O my Lord! I seek Your refuge from the promptings of the devils, and I seek Your refuge from their presence near me.

(Sūra al-Mu'minūn 23:97-98)

〰 **Can you think back to times when you have let Shaytan get the better of you?**

〰 **How will you advise your children about friends and frenemies?**

_____

_____

_____

_____

_____

31. WHY SO SERIOUS?

وُجُوهٌ يَوْمَئِذٍ نَاعِمَةٌ. لِسَعْيِهَا رَاضِيَةٌ.

Some faces on that day will be joyous; pleased with their endeavour.

(Sūra al-Ghāshiya 88:8)

'But what's wrong, Mummy?' my oldest daughter asked with concern. 'Nothing', I replied. She wouldn't let it go, and asked again, 'Then why do you look annoyed?' 'Annoyed?' I retorted, 'I'm not annoyed. I'm busy, but not annoyed.' In my typical busy frenzy, I had not realized that I had been wearing a frown on my face most of the day, moving from one task to another in single-minded concentration with a deeply furrowed brow. I was on a mission and had lots of work to do, and whizzed from one task to the other, oblivious to what my face looked like to my kids. My game face apparently looked 'annoyed' even though I was far from annoyed that particular day.

As mums, our to-do lists are never ending, and it seems that there is more on the list at the end of the day than when we began. In our fervour to get everything done, we overlook how we go about doing it. I am certainly not suggesting we constantly whistle while we work or go around the house with a smile plastered across our faces whilst doing homework with our kids, as more often than not, it's serious work we are doing. In the same token though, it is important that we do not take ourselves too seriously. My daughter's observation was a timely reminder of this for me: that in all my seriousness, busyness and stress of mothering, I had forgotten to be cheerful and have fun with them. Our children are very sensitive to joy, and pick up on the lack of it very quickly. They need our light-heartedness as much as they need our love, and they thrive when they see us having fun right alongside them. No amount of busyness is worth missing the time to laugh, joke around, get on the floor and wrestle with them or just smile at them from time to time.

I had learned many strategies for making a cheerful home and being jovial with the children from an excellent book called *Playful Parenting* by Lawrence Cohen. He suggests various things from using a silly voice to cheer a sad child up: "Turn that frown upside down", to saying in our gloomiest and sternest voice, 'This is a very serious and solemn occasion' whilst keeping a straight face. To date, we have never managed to say that phrase with a straight face without bursting into giggles! My children have always loved it when I have gotten down on the floor to play with them, turned a chore into a game or a race, acted silly with them, or just flashed them a cheesy smile!

The problem was that I had forgotten to use these strategies recently, and needed to unearth them and use them to make my home light-hearted and cheerful again. We often teach our children about how smiley the Prophet (pbuh) was, or how much he enjoyed playing games with his grandchildren, letting them ride on his back, cheering them on in wrestling matches, or racing with them. These aspects of his example are all part of his sunnah too, for us to follow, especially since he has taught us, *"You will not be able to encompass all people with your money, so meet them with cheerful faces and joy."* (al-Kāfī, v.2, p.103, no.1)

Our to-do lists are not going to get any shorter, but our days of fun and laughter with our children will fly past in the blink of an eye. If we are not mindful, our home can be at risk of becoming a crabby and moody environment where our children then crave to go out for all their fun and entertainment. It is up to us to set the tone and mood in our homes. I, for one, would love for my children to see their home as a fun and inviting place to be and where their parents are warm and cheerful. I just have to work on reminding myself to turn my own frown upside down!

اللَّهُمَّ اجْعَلْ فِي قَلْبِي نُورًا وَفِي بَصَرِي نُورًا وَفِي سَمْعِي نُورًا

وَعَنْ يَمِينِي نُورًا وَعَنْ يَسَارِي نُورًا وَفَوْقِي نُورًا وَتَحْتِي نُورًا

وَأَمَامِي نُورًا وَخَلْفِي نُورًا وَاجْعَلْ لِي نُورًا.

O Allah, place light for me in my heart, light in my sight, light in my hearing, light to my right and to my left, light above me and below me, light in front of me and behind me, and give me light.

(Supplication taught by the Prophet (pbuh) asking Allah
to make us 'light'-hearted)

ℳ If you were to ask your children to describe the mood in
   your home, what one word do you think they would use?

ℳ What is the greatest thief of cheerfulness in your home
   right now?

ℳ What are some ways in which you could bring more cheer
   and fun into your home?

32. BUT EVERYONE'S DOING IT

وَمَنْ أَحْسَنُ دِيْنًا مِمَّنْ أَسْلَمَ وَجْهَهُ للهِ وَهُوَ مُحْسِنٌ واتَّبَعَ مِلَّةَ
إِبْرَاهِيْمَ حَنِيْفًا وَاتَّخَذَ اللهُ إِبْرَاهِيْمَ خَلِيْلًا.

*And who has a better path than he who submits his will to God, being
virtuous, and follows the creed of Ibrahim, upright? And God took
Ibrahim as a dedicated friend.*

(Sūra al-Nisāʾ: 125)

My friend's voice quivered on the phone, as she proceeded to tell
me how her 11 year-old son had been pressurised by his friends into
watching porn on an iPad that one of the boys had sneaked onto the
coach on a school trip. 'He said he felt disgusted, but couldn't really do
anything about it. He was too scared to rat them out to the teacher and
get them into trouble, and now they're making fun of him because he
closed his eyes!' We talked at length, reassuring each other that at least
our children had a sense of shame, and communicated with us about
these things. We discussed what steps we could take to speak to the
school, and to protect them from such things in the future. My friend
wasn't Muslim, and whilst we differed on issues like sleepovers and
gender interactions, we shared the same worries about peer pressure
and the impending doom of all the challenges that were yet to come:
pressures to dress or talk a certain way, buy into expensive brands,
truancy, shoplifting, pornography, dating, parties, alcohol, drugs and
other experimentation. Nobody likes the thought of being influenced
to do anything against their will, let alone their children.

We certainly weren't ostriches, and we acknowledged that the
peer pressure had already begun (many years ago, actually) and they
weren't even in high school yet. That cesspool, and beyond, was going

to be wholly different. We had been through it as teenagers ourselves, but the world was a far more dangerous place now, and we couldn't leave our children at the mercy of chance, that they would not succumb to these pressures. Even though we, and our spouses, both came from close-knit home environments, had good social circles, and for now, we liked to believe that our children would always choose the right path, we felt it would be a good idea to have a practical plan in place. As adults, we are prone to be in sticky situations at some point in our lives, and children more so, so it made sense to prepare them and ourselves for what was yet to come. Below are 7 tips and pointers that have worked for us collectively over the years:

1) Teach them from young to be comfortable in their own skins - as Muslims in our case - with their own unique talents and skills, their own likes and dislikes. Marketing of popular culture starts very very young, and children feel the pressure of owning merchandise from their favourite shows very early on. I remember my son had never even watched a single episode of Teenage Mutant Ninja Turtles but felt compelled to have the lunchbox because his friends had it! As harmless as a lunchbox is, it is important to teach them that they equally have the power to influence others positively and can be trend-setters too, that people are free to have their own likes and dislikes and that it's okay to be different to their peers and still enjoy each other's company. And it's also okay not to be liked by everyone all of the time.

2) It is paramount that our own language and behaviour does not betray any excessive concern for people's opinions or to conform to other people's standards. Are we embarrassed to excuse ourselves to go and pray during an event? Do we loosen our own principles when we are with a certain peer group? Our children watch all this, so it is important to be mindful of what subtle messages we give them.

3) Different children will respond differently to suggestions and pressure from their friends. Just because you have verbally taught

them from young, does not mean that they will not be susceptible or tempted. Just because they are raised in a Muslim household or come from a Muslim background does not mean that they are immune to anything. Your one child may have sailed through their teenage years without even wanting to imitate her peers or toe the line with anything remotely questionable, whilst your second may be experimentative and easily influenced, wanting to test every boundary. Be prepared for this.

4) Teach children from young that it's fine to say NO to things that make them feel uncomfortable, whether it's hugging somebody they don't want to, or trying something that they are averse to. If we too often tell children that it's rude to say no, or that it'll look bad, or that they *have to*, they will grow up being reluctant to say no, even when it matters. We need to teach them that their gut instincts are valuable, and how to say 'No' politely. As a Yes-person myself, I struggled with saying 'No' until well into adulthood. Sharing stories of situations that we faced growing up - and courageously surmounted - can be a lot more effective than lecturing them about such things. It also imparts to them that we understand what they are going through.

5) It goes without saying that the right choice of friends is crucial. The Qur'an is replete with advice and admonition about types of people to befriend and who to stay away from, and puts down the wrong choice of friend as one of our biggest regrets on the Day of Judgment: 'And the day when the wrongdoer shall bite his hands saying, "Oh if only I had taken a path with the Messenger. Woe betide me! If only I had not taken so and so for a friend!"' (Sūra al-Furqān: 27-28). Interestingly, God uses the same word for friend 'khalīl' as an honorific to describe Prophet Ibrahim (pbuh) and that He adopted him as a 'friend', precisely due to his uprightness and his refusal to conform to his peers' idolatrous norms at the time. God praises him many times as being *ḥanīf*: 'steadfast' in the face of pressure, even from his own family. The Prophet (pbuh) too, advised us to carefully consider our friends, since their way of life becomes ours: *'Man follows*

the same creed as his friend, so consider carefully who it is you befriend.'
Again, whilst we cannot orchestrate our children's friendships beyond
a certain age, we can certainly advise them.

6) X-Plan: I came across a strategy called X-Plan, devised by a
parent in the US who works with youth addiction recovery groups.
He found through his experience working with teens that almost all
of them only stayed in sticky situations because they felt like they did
not have a way out. So he came up with the X-Plan for his family: a
lifeline or rehearsed way-out plan for sticky situations that his teens
may find themselves in. If the teenager was ever to find herself in a
sticky situation where she needed a way out, she simply had to secretly
text X to one of her parents or older siblings, who would then call her
right back, talking loud enough for her peers to overhear, with the
pretext of an emergency at home for which she was going to be picked
up immediately. At that point, the teen could inform her friends that
something had happened at home, due to which she had to leave.

In short, when stuck in tight spot, she knows she has a way out,
whilst having no pressure to open herself up to social ridicule, and
giving herself time and space to think about the situation. She has
the freedom to protect herself while continuing to grow and learn to
navigate this world. This also opens up judgment-free conversation
afterwards and builds trust between parents and their teens, where
eventually their immediate reaction when stuck in a tight spot
will not be: 'Mum's gonna kill me' but rather: 'I need to call Mum'.
Moreover, it presents an opportunity for us as parents to teach our
children that they can be honest (something DID come up, and they
DO have to leave), while learning that it's okay to be guarded in how
much they reveal to others. They don't owe anyone an explanation the
next day, and if asked can give the honest answer, "It's private and I
don't want to talk about it" until they feel strong enough to stand by
their principles.

Of course, the ideal response would be to boldly stand up to them as modelled by Prophet Ibrahim (pbuh), but this is not always possible if they are caught unaware, find themselves in danger or outnumbered, or if they fear repercussions to their stance at the time, or are simply not confident enough in their principles. And often the best course of action is physical distance from the situation as fast as possible. This is simply an emergency safety net for our children as we continue to communicate and nurture valuable skills in them. And we must remember: they are far more likely to give in to the peer pressure if they fear dire and punitive consequences at home.

7) And last, but by no means least, we have been blessed beyond our fathoming, with supplications for protection against such negative influences, and taught exactly how to beseech God in such situations. Who better to seek refuge in when seeking protection from people's negative influences than the very Maker of those people, their King, and their God.

قُلْ أَعُوذُ بِرَبِّ النَّاسِ ﴿١﴾ مَلِكِ النَّاسِ ﴿٢﴾ إِلَـٰهِ النَّاسِ ﴿٣﴾

مِن شَرِّ الْوَسْوَاسِ الْخَنَّاسِ ﴿٤﴾

الَّذِي يُوَسْوِسُ فِي صُدُورِ النَّاسِ ﴿٥﴾ مِنَ الْجِنَّةِ وَالنَّاسِ ﴿٦﴾

Say: I seek refuge with the Nurturer of mankind, the King of mankind, the God of mankind, from the evil of the retreating whisperer, who whispers into the breasts of mankind, from among the jinn and mankind.

(Sūra 114: al-Nās)

≫ Can you think back to when you faced peer pressure as a teenager? How did you handle the situation?

≫ Have you or your children ever been roped into doing something where you wished you had been able to say NO? What could you do differently next time?

_____

_____

_____

_____

_____

_____

_____

_____

_____

_____

_____

33. LOWER YOUR WINGS, BABY BIRD

وَاخْفِضْ لَهُمَا جَنَاحَ الذُّلِّ مِنَ الرَّحْمَةِ...

And lower to them the wing of humility out of mercy...

(Sūra al-Isrāʾ 17:24)

Respect to Parents was the title of an annually recurring topic in our Sunday School manuals when we were growing up, with increasing detail and information added on each year. I distinctly remember one of them having a little word-search related to the topic and a *hadith* in big bold print: *"Even if you come before Allah with all the good deeds of all the prophets, you will not even be able to smell paradise if you have disrespected your parents."* It must have been effective to have stuck with me well into adulthood. Respect to Parents is the *akhlaq* lesson that I remember being the most emphasised and the most reiterated from my teachers, the pulpit, and from the lips of my own parents: 'Don't even say *uff* to them', 'Don't roll your eyes at them', 'Raising your voice to your parent is a grave sin (*kabīra*)', 'Beware of upsetting them', and all the myriad stories that accompanied, like the man who went for Hajj with his mother on his back to try to repay one night of her rocking him to sleep, and the young man who was to be Prophet Musa's neighbour for his kind treatment of his elderly mother – there are so many examples.

Although true to the core, when hearing it from my own parents' mouths as a teenager, it felt a lot like they were guilt-tripping me at the time, and at every opportunity. And now as a parent myself, it makes me rethink the best way forward to impart this extremely important lesson to my own children without it coming across as preachy and self-serving. My parents had the advantage of Gujrati on their side, which we spoke exclusively at home. Like many eastern and western languages, it has a separate pronoun for 'you' when addressing adults, *'taméh'* (equivalent to the French *vous*) which commands more respect than just the English universal 'you'. So when addressing them, it was almost impossible to use the respectable *'taméh'* while saying something disrespectful in the same breath. My sisters and I dared not question their better judgment, or ask why we had do something now rather than later, or say 'But you don't understand!' which, from my children's English mouths comes out quite effortlessly! My own children in contrast - simply by virtue of their language - come across as master negotiators and quite brazen, barring any disrespect in the content. So how to impart these all-important teachings to them when the topic of 'Respect to Parents' still echoes in my ears with a list of 'don'ts' rather than a positive list of what to 'do' instead.

Parents is a subject dealt with neutrally in the Qur'an through both positive commands and prohibitions: 'Don't say *uff*', but also 'Treat them with kindness' juxtaposed to God's own obedience (Sūra al-Isrā' 17:23), along with many supplications for them. The command quoted in the verse above has always fascinated me: *'Lower to them the wing of humility out of mercy'*. We are told to lower our wings towards fellow believers too, but for parents God specifies 'the wing of humility' and further adds 'out of mercy'. What does He mean by lowering our wings to them, and why use feathery 'wings', when He could have used human faculties like lower your voice or your head?

A bird's wings represent its ability to fly, its freedom and independence, its power to roam the world and fend for itself. Our parents are the ones who strengthened our wings when we were baby birds, nourished our bodies, fed us from their own mouths, and nurtured our abilities to fly out into the world in independence. When God tells us to lower our wings, He is reminding us to come back down to earth when we are with our parents. He knows that we can fly, He knows what we are capable of, how educated and successful we are. But when we are with our parents, we are to act as if we do not have wings. We must lower them out of mercy for them. Be humble before them. Act as is we are their chicks, still needy of them, even if just in principle; chicks who listen to their advice attentively, who concede that mum and dad know better, even as CEOs and great educators ourselves.

Wings also represent protection from the elements. Just as they protected us with their great wings when we were mere goslings and eaglets, so must we now lower our wings protectively over them as they age. They now have fears, which to us in our prime may seem irrational: fear of losing their memory, fear of falling, of burglars, of open spaces, of enclosed spaces, crowds, getting lost, loneliness, people's comments, ill health, and so on. Just as they allayed all our fears and protected us from them, and from many other very real dangers as we were growing up, so must we do the same for them.

God does not paint a metaphorical picture for us to marvel at His beautiful imagery and poetic prowess, but so that we may think about it and put it into practice. The very best way our children will learn this essential life lesson - which ultimately will be for our benefit in our old age anyway - is for them to see us lowering our wings of humility out of mercy towards their grandparents, treating them with kindness, praying for them, going out of our way to serve them, and going above and beyond the mere call of duty.

وَقُل رَّبِّ ارْحَمْهُمَا كَمَا رَبَّيَانِي صَغِيرًا. ...

...and say: My Lord! Have mercy on them as they brought me up when I was small

(Sūra al-Isrāʾ:24 - continuation of the above command to lower our wings)

- How do the lessons in respecting parents that you learned growing up impact the way you now impart it to your children?

- Is there room for improvement in your relationship with your parents?

- What practical steps could you take to model 'lowering the wing of humility to your parents' for your children?

34. A SIGHT FOR SORE EYES

فَرَدَدْنَاهُ إِلَىٰ أُمِّهِ كَيْ تَقَرَّ عَيْنُهَا وَلَا تَحْزَنَ وَلِتَعْلَمَ أَنَّ وَعْدَ اللَّهِ حَقٌّ وَلَٰكِنَّ أَكْثَرَهُمْ لَا يَعْلَمُونَ.

So we returned him to his mother so that she might be comforted and not grieve, and that she might know that Allah's promise is true, but most of them do not know.

(Sūra Qaṣaṣ 28:13)

Qurratul ʿayn is a beautiful idiomatic expression in Arabic meaning 'coolness of the eye' and is used for something that fills you with joy and delight, like seeing your child return from a journey, or coming home to smiling children after a long day at work. An English equivalent might be 'a sight for sore eyes' or 'the apple of my eye'. The opposite is also used in Arabic - warmth of the eye, where one might cry hot tears of anger or grief, when saying goodbye to a loved one for example, or when extremely angry or upset. The actual root of the word *qurrat* is *qa-rra* which means to settle or fix, so it also has the notion of fixing one's gaze on something, or the English equivalent of 'being unable to take one's eyes off something' because it is so beautiful and captivating.

Qurratul ʿayn is what Lady Fatima (pbuh) is reported to have called her children in endearment in Hadith al-Kisa: *'qurrata ʿaynī wa thamarata fuʾādī'* - 'the coolness of my eye and the fruit of my heart'. It is so sweet to think that Imam Hasan and Imam Husayn (pbut) delighted her eyes so much and that she could not take her eyes off them. This phrase, however, has precedent in the Qur'an itself, and God uses the expression in many places. Interestingly, He uses it in the stories of Lady Maryam, Asiya and Yukabad. In the verse above, when Prophet Musa's mother, Yukabad, throws him in the river to save him from Fir'awn who has issued a command for all Israelite baby boys to be killed, she is filled with anguish and anxiety. Allah says, *'We returned him to his mother so that 'her eyes may be cooled'* - literally - *and she would not grieve'*. It was not enough for her to simply be told that the baby was doing fine in the palace and that they had not harmed him. Fixating her gaze upon her baby was the antidote necessary for her grief.

Similarly, Lady Maryam (pbuh) as soon as she gives birth to Prophet Isa is told to eat, drink and fill your eyes with the sight of him in the verse: *"So eat and drink, and refresh your eyes (by looking at him)..."* (Sūra Maryam 19:26). Gazing at her baby was a necessary process in her recovery, as basic as eating and drinking. Asiya uses the phrase very skilfully in her bid to get Fir'awn to adopt baby Musa (pbuh). She knew very well that it was dangerous for this baby to be in the palace with all these blood-thirsty henchmen present, and yet she boldly took him to Fir'awn and said: *qurratu 'aynin lī wa laka'* - 'a sight for my sore eyes and yours' (Sūra al-Qaṣaṣ 28:9). She obviously thought he was cute, but she made Fir'awn look at him too, as if to say, 'Awww, you think he's cute, don't you?' It's astonishing: how could a tyrant, hell-bent on killing baby boys, change his mind and desist even though the very target of his vendetta was right on his lap? This baby definitely looked different to the Egyptian babies. He was of a different race altogether, but Fir'awn seems to have been blind to his skin colour and race, and saw only his cuteness, succumbing to Asiya's audacious suggestion of adopting him as a son! How was fixing his gaze on a cute little baby that powerful that it could prevent him from killing him?

The answer: oxytocin, a.k.a. the love hormone. It is only in the modern era of scientific development that we now understand the role of the hormone oxytocin that surges and is released upon childbirth and nursing, and contributes to creating the bond between mother and child, and even father and child - yes, dads release it too - and even non-parents in small doses when they see cute babies or baby animals, as part of God's special evolutionary mechanism to ensure the survival of infants. An all-important factor that stimulates its release, in addition to nursing and skin to skin contact, is simply gazing at the sweet newborn. There are numerous studies that have researched and tested this phenomenon, but God documents it in the Qur'an for us, which is why Lady Maryam is told to gaze at her baby. The surge of oxytocin is also a great help against postnatal depression as other hormones plummet and cause overwhelm and a sense of deflation in the new mother, and the Qur'an explicitly tells us: *"We returned him to his mother so that her eyes may be cooled by looking at him and so that she would not grieve"*.

That is why maternal recovery after birth is of utmost importance. Yes, we live in busy times where household chores beckon, and older children have to be dropped to school and people do not have the luxury of living in extended families, but the Qur'anic wisdom of allowing a mother time to recover and enjoy looking at her baby still rings true. The role of mothers and mother-in-laws, family, close friends, and doulas cannot be overemphasised in supporting the new parents and allowing them time to recover and enjoy the baby. Celebrity culture gives us a very wrong view of mothers being able to bounce back to work straight after birth, but this is not how our Maker has designed us. Bouncing back to cooking and cleaning, or going to work is not a competition, and there is much wisdom in Eastern cultures' 40-day rule of new mothers being looked after and not allowed to go out for six weeks postpartum. The physical, mental and emotional wellbeing of both mother and baby, and even the father for that matter, could do with a dose of 40-day care in our fast-paced lives. We may live in different times but the natural needs of human beings and their babies have not changed, and parental bonding is as essential as it has always been. Bringing new life into this world is a miraculous event and needs to be treated as such.

رَبَّنَا هَبْ لَنَا مِنْ أَزْوَاجِنَا وَذُرِّيَّاتِنَا قُرَّةَ أَعْيُنٍ وَاجْعَلْنَا لِلْمُتَّقِينَ إِمَامًا.

Our Lord, delight our eyes through our spouses and offspring, and make us leaders of the God-conscious.

(Sūra Furqān 25:74)

It has been narrated that Imam Ali (pbuh) often used to recite this Qur'anic supplication, where we ask Allah to make our children and spouses 'the coolness of our eyes', such that we find delight and joy in looking at them.

⟫⟫⟋ **Were you lucky enough to have time to enjoy gazing at your baby after he/she was born? Do you remember the feelings that created in you?**

⟫⟫⟋ **Think of ways in which you might be able to support another new mum after childbirth so she can enjoy the same time with her baby without pressure?**

_____

_____

_____

_____

_____

_____

35. GLORY IN THE ORDINARY

وَمَا أَرْسَلْنَا قَبْلَكَ مِنَ الْمُرْسَلِينَ إِلَّا إِنَّهُمْ لَيَأْكُلُونَ الطَّعَامَ وَيَمْشُونَ فِي الْأَسْوَاقِ ۗ وَجَعَلْنَا بَعْضَكُمْ لِبَعْضٍ فِتْنَةً أَتَصْبِرُونَ ۗ وَكَانَ رَبُّكَ بَصِيرًا.

We did not send any messengers before you but that they indeed ate food and walked in marketplaces. We have made you a [means of] test for one another, [to see] if you will be patient and steadfast, and your Lord is all-Seeing.

(Sūra al-Furqān:20)

Reading about the prophets' and infallible Imams' lives, their immaculate characters, and their illuminated faces, has always made me wonder why more people were not attracted to their message. They are described as guiding lamps and shining lights, and yet why were more people not drawn to their glow from far and wide? Why did people around them not treat them with more reverence? This has been an age-old test: for people to believe in a messenger who walks in the marketplaces and eats food just like them, and is quite ordinary on the surface. Although naturally charismatic, messengers were never designed to be glamorous. They attracted people purely through the truth of their message and their good conduct. They were glorious in their very ordinariness. Just like us mothers.

Motherhood, especially when mothering little ones, is not stylish, glitzy or glamorous. If motherhood were personified, she would likely be messy, gooey, smelling of burp cloths and explosive nappies, and wearing a stained shirt. The closest to glamorous and glittery we mothers get is glitter-glue stuck to our carpets! Sometimes what is supposed to be our 'great feat' of raising human beings feels anything but great, and when we're frantically running around doing the routine school drops, fuelled only by coffee and carbs, it feels anything but special and important. Yes, motherhood is gruelling, gritty, and grimy but definitely not glamorous.

And yet God, the all-Seeing and all-Aware, has promised us glorious rewards for that very ordinary-looking task of bringing up human beings. The Prophet (pbuh), addressing women in his community, said, *'Does it not please you (O Women!) that when you conceive from your husbands while he is pleased with you, then that woman will receive such reward equal to that of a fasting person in the path of Allah and spending the night in worship. When her labour pains commence the inhabitants of the earth and the sky are unaware of the stores of comfort that are prepared for her. When she delivers and breastfeeds her child then she will be granted a reward for every gulp of milk, and if she has to remain awake during the night for the sake of her child, she will receive the reward of emancipating seventy slaves in the path of Allah.'*

His definition of extraordinary and special is very different to ours. His special chosen ones, though quite mediocre and ordinary in appearance to their contemporaries on the outside, radiated His grace. God has a way of turning the ordinary into extraordinary. When Prophet Musa (pbuh) went up to Mount Sinai to talk to God, God asked him, 'What is that in your right hand, Musa?' Prophet Musa replied, 'This is my staff: I recline on it and I beat the leaves with it so they fall upon my sheep, and I have other uses for it too.' (Sūra Ṭāhā 20:17-18). As much as Prophet Musa (pbuh) was extolling the virtues of his plain, wooden staff - maybe in his nervous bid to lengthen his conversation with His Creator - at the end of the day, it was just an ordinary stick. But God transformed that same staff into a miraculous, venomous serpent that exposed wrongdoers' lies.

Did Hajar, the black slave concubine wife of Prophet Ibrahim (pbuh) - even less than ordinary in her time - have any idea, when she persisted in her maternally instinctive and frenzied search for water to save her baby's life, desperately running back and forth between the hills of Safa and Marwa, that millions of pilgrims for thousands of years would follow in her footsteps? There were no witnesses around, no radio broadcasts, no cameras catching her in the act but God's watchful Eye and His Power to transform the mediocre into magnificent. Similarly, He turned barren old women such as Sara and Prophet Zakariyya's wife into child-bearing mothers. And of course, He created us: wondrously complex human beings from an ordinary lump of clay. That is His way.

We may never experience celebrity status, fame, fortune or glamour of any kind in this world in our very ordinary role as mothers, but in God's Eyes, we are special due to our spacious hearts, our unselfish love, our extraordinary endurance and our fantastic faith in our commitment to raising our children well. People's standards of measuring worth can be so shallow, based on looks, sporting ability, talents, wealth, and status – many of which are often inherited or God-given. God, however, measures our worth by what is squarely in our control: our deeds, and more important than that, the hidden intentions behind our deeds. Sometimes our mothering efforts can seem insignificant compared to celebrated public campaigns of good-doing, but Allah has a special place for the uncelebrated workers who work hard sincerely behind closed doors, without praise, 'likes' or awards. He tells them encouragingly, 'Keep working, for Allah will see your work...' (Sūra al-Tawba 9:105) and: 'For everyone there are degrees [of merit] pertaining to what he has done: He will recompense them fully for their works, and they will not be wronged.' (Sūra al-Aḥqāf 46:19)

At times when we feel anything but special, it is important to remind ourselves that Paradise lies right under our calloused, tired feet, albeit allegorically. Outsiders may not be attracted to our grisly, messy motherhood moments, but God and our children love us in our glorious ordinariness without bling, make up and accolades, just as we are.

إِلَهِي كَيْفَ أَدْعُوكَ وَ أَنَا وَ كَيْفَ أَقْطَعُ رَجَائِي مِنْكَ وَ أَنْتَ أَنْتَ

إِلَهِي إِذَا لَمْ أَسْأَلْكَ فَتُعْطِيَنِي فَمَنْ ذَا الَّذِي أَسْأَلُهُ فَيُعْطِينِي

إِلَهِي إِذَا لَمْ أَدْعُكَ فَتَسْتَجِيبَ لِي فَمَنْ ذَا الَّذِي أَدْعُوهُ فَيَسْتَجِيبُ لِي

إِلَهِي إِذَا لَمْ أَتَضَرَّعْ إِلَيْكَ فَتَرْحَمَنِي فَمَنْ ذَا الَّذِي أَتَضَرَّعُ إِلَيْهِ
فَيَرْحَمُنِي

إِلَهِي فَكَمَا فَلَقْتَ الْبَحْرَ لِمُوسَى عَلَيْهِ السَّلَامُ وَ نَجَّيْتَهُ

أَسْأَلُكَ أَنْ تُصَلِّيَ عَلَى مُحَمَّدٍ وَ آلِهِ

وَ أَنْ تُنْجِّيَنِي مِمَّا أَنَا فِيهِ وَ تُفَرِّجَ عَنِّي فَرَجاً عَاجِلاً غَيْرَ آجِلٍ

بِفَضْلِكَ وَ رَحْمَتِكَ يَا أَرْحَمَ الرَّاحِمِينَ.

My God how can I call on You when I am (insignificant) me?
And yet how can I cut off hope from You when You are (Awesome)
You? My God, if I do not beseech You in order that You give to me,
then who am I going to beseech to give to me?
My God, if I don't call You that You may respond to me,
then who can I call who will respond to me?
My God if I do not beg from You to have mercy on me,
then who can I beg from to have mercy on me?
My God I beseech You that just as You parted the sea for Musa (peace
be on him) and saved him, so send blessings on Muhammad and on
the children of Muhammad, and come to my rescue, and deliver me
(from these troubles), and grant me relief,
and do it quickly, without delay, through Your kindness and Your
mercy, O the most Merciful.

(Duʿa' *Ilāhī Kayfa Adʿūka* for speedy fulfilment of all legitimate desires)

〰️ Have you felt stuck in the ordinariness of mothering this week? What did you do to help yourself out of feeling this way?

〰️ Name one ordinary task that you have to complete today. How could you realign your thinking about it to see it as a glorious offering rather than an uncelebrated chore?

36. THE DREADED 'D' WORD

وَمَن يَتَّقِ اللَّهَ يَجْعَل لَّهُ مَخْرَجًا ﴿٢﴾ وَيَرْزُقْهُ مِنْ حَيْثُ لَا يَحْتَسِبُ ۚ وَمَن يَتَوَكَّلْ عَلَى اللَّهِ فَهُوَ حَسْبُهُ ۚ إِنَّ اللَّهَ بَالِغُ أَمْرِهِ ۚ قَدْ جَعَلَ اللَّهُ لِكُلِّ شَيْءٍ قَدْرًا ﴿٣﴾

Whoever is wary of [his duty to] Allah, He will make a way out for him; and provide for him from whence he does not count upon. And whoever puts his trust in Allah, He will suffice him. Indeed Allah carries through His commands.
Certainly, Allah has ordained a measure [and extent] for everything.

(Sūra al-Ṭalāq 65:2-3)

The above verses of the Qur'an are hands-down one of my favourite verses, if not my favourite, which I have resorted to for strength and reassurance many many times in my life. Many people are familiar with them as the 'Verses of 1000 Dinars', purported by some narrations to exponentially increase in one's *rizq* (sustenance) when recited daily after *fajr* as was reportedly taught by Khidr to a poor man who experienced great wealth thereafter. Many people thus hang it in their houses or shops, and one scholar even remarked, after witnessing its effectiveness, that it should have been called the 'Verse of 1 Million Dinars' since Allah is so infinitely Generous.

It has also popularly come to be known as the 'Better than Alchemy' verse, after Imam Khomeini was taught it within a powerful formula by the great scholar and spiritual wayfarer Haaj Nokhudaki. Imam Khomeini asked the scholar to teach him the secret of alchemy if he knew it, by the honour of Imam al-Ridha (pbuh) in whose courtyard they were standing. Haaj Nokhudaki replied that he could teach him something even better than alchemy if he could promise to guard this knowledge, use it appropriately and not abuse it. Imam Khomeini, being a man of scrupulous honesty, admitted that he could not promise that. When he heard this, Haaj Nokhudaki turned to him and said, "Since you admit that you are unable to guard the knowledge of alchemy, I will teach you something even better than alchemy, and that is:

After every *wajib salat*, recite Ayat al-Kursi until (وَهُـوَ الْعَـلِيُّ الْعَظِيـمُ) once, then recite the *tasbih* of Lady Fatima (A), then recite Sūra al-Tawḥīd three times, then recite the Salawat three times, then recite the second and third verses of Sūra al-Ṭalāq three times. And this is better for you than alchemy."

I can't speak for alchemy or even fathom what that kind of knowledge looks like, but I have certainly found these verses to be extremely beneficial in my own life, as you may have too. Whilst these reports and much anecdotal evidence from people's lives and experiences have brought these verses to the forefront as conducive to increased *rizq* and knowledge, and a help against misfortunes, what is not commonly known or discussed is the context of these verses in the Qur'an. They are found in Sūra al-Ṭalāq (Divorce) where God commands the believers to be just and kind in their treatment of their wives when they divorce them, and about the laws of the prescribed waiting period. It comes as a reassurance to both men and women that if they are conscious of their duty to God and trust in Him fully, He will make a way out of their situation for them, and provide for them from sources unimaginable.

The D word is unsettling at best, especially when there are children in a marriage, but sometimes we can be faced with struggles and difficulties beyond our control, and the strife and conflict is no longer manageable. Whilst the remit of this book is not marriage or separation advice, nor to discuss the legal or moralistic causes or ramifications of divorce, nor even to go into a rights debate, what must be highlighted is that the impact on children cannot be underestimated. The steps towards a permanent separation between spouses have to be well calculated, and the consequences carefully considered and mitigated as best as possible. When children are involved, it is no longer a case of spouses divorcing, but *parents*; and this has to be borne in mind before making any sort of haste with such a weighty decision, unless of course the children or spouse's immediate wellbeing is at stake.

It undeniably has an effect on children in even the most well-managed of divorces, and in that respect, men - whom God has designated to be the maintainers of women and children (usually the ones who stand to be worst affected) - must ensure that their dependants receive their right to financial and emotional security.

Nonetheless, our Compassionate, All-seeing Lord has made divorce permissible and has devoted a whole *sūra* and many verses to its treatment, precisely so that people do not abuse it, and threaten divorce in anger. Divorce can unhinge even the mildest-mannered people, and even the most balanced of them can become unsettled.

Before Allah makes any promises to provide for us and make a way out for us, He first makes it conditional upon us being conscious and wary of our duty to Him (*taqwā*) and that He is watching our dealings at all times. The word *yattaqī* in the verse, and *taqwā*, come from the root *wa-qā,* which essentially means to guard or protect ourselves from any wrongdoing, and from the consequences of our actions. Keeping our faith strong, adhering to Him, being honest with ourselves and our spouses, persevering, and maintaining dignity and decency in such tempestuous situations is a real challenge. It can be quite easy to lose faith and to resort to wrongdoing in our anger, frustration and trauma.

Hence God's advice - to both men and women - to first be God-conscious, followed by trusting in Him alone. When we do this, and rely on Him fully with conviction that His provision will come, even from indirect means, supplicating Him fervently and sincerely, then He is enough for us and will never abandon us. And His promise is always true.

اَللَّهُمَّ صَلِّ عَلَىٰ مُحَمَّدٍ وَآلِ مُحَمَّدٍ وَأَجْعَلْ لِي مِنْ أَمْرِي فَرَجاً وَمَخْرَجاً وَأَرْزُقْنِي مِنْ حَيْثُ أَحْتَسِبُ وَمِنْ حَيْثُ لاَ أَحْتَسِبُ.

O Allah, bless Muḥammmad and the family of Muḥammad, and give me relief and a way out for me in all my affairs, and provide for me from whence I expect as well as whence I do not expect.

(Supplication recommended after *fajr* for relief from difficult situations)

≫ In what tumultuous challenges in your life have you directly experienced Allah's help and provision from sources unimaginable?

≫ How could being God-conscious help you deal with difficult situations in your own marriage?

37. THE TWO WORDS FOR 'PARENTS' IN ARABIC

وَقَضَىٰ رَبُّكَ أَلَّا تَعْبُدُوا إِلَّا إِيَّاهُ وَبِالْوَالِدَيْنِ إِحْسَانًا ۚ إِمَّا يَبْلُغَنَّ عِندَكَ الْكِبَرَ أَحَدُهُمَا أَوْ كِلَاهُمَا فَلَا تَقُل لَّهُمَا أُفٍّ وَلَا تَنْهَرْهُمَا وَقُل لَّهُمَا قَوْلًا كَرِيمًا.

And your Lord has decreed that you not worship except Him, and good treatment of parents. Whether one or both of them reach old age [while] with you, say not to them [so much as], "uff," and do not repel them but speak to them a kind word.

(Sūra al-Isrā' 17:23)

The precision of the Arabic language is marvellous. Take the singular and plural, for example. In English and in most other languages, we have a singular, for example, house, and then two or more of that thing are plural: houses. In Arabic, there is a separate label or word for two things, expressed by the dual, then three and above are plural. Although there are other languages that have used the dual such as Ancient Greek, Sanskrit, Slavic languages and even Old English, Arabic is probably the only language that still actively uses it, both classical and modern Arabic. Words that are dual in meaning, such as: 2 gardens or 2 houses end in the sound *'aan'* or *'ayn'*. So when people refer to the *zohr* and *asr* prayers together, they say *zohrayn*, i.e. the two afternoon prayers, or when Imams Hasan and Husayn (pbut) are referred to together, we say Hasanayn, i.e. 'the two Hasans'.

Parents are referred to by two different dual words in the Qur'an: *abawayn* (literally: 'two fathers') and *wālidayn*. I have always wondered why God uses both these words to refer to parents. What was the difference between them, if any, since the word *wālid* is also used for father, like *ab*? When researching, I found that He uses *abawayn* when discussing matters related to inheritance, parental authority, and stating parental relationships as a matter of fact, such as when referring to Adam and Eve as our parents, or referring to Prophet Yusuf's parents. The word *wālidayn* He uses in all prophetic supplications of Prophet Sulayman and Prophet Ibrahim for their parents when they would ask God to forgive them, whenever God himself commands us to treat them kindly, deal justly with them, thank them, spend benevolently on them, and any other injunction involving kindness or mercy. So there clearly was a difference in their usage, but where did this differentiation stem from?

When digging deeper, I discovered that it all boils down to the root of those words. The root of the word '*wālid*' is *wa-la-da* which means to give birth. A *wālid* is used to mean father, but he does not actually give birth. He is called a *wālid*, because he is the male counterpart of the *wālida*, the mother who actually gives birth. It is her action of bringing life into this world that warrants the title *wālid* for the father, and *wālidayn* for them both. Giving birth is the action that warrants prayers, supplication and command of kindness to them. For everything else related to parental authority and systematic aspects of parenting, *abawayn* - linked to the actual word for 'father' - is used because the family unit is seen as largely patriarchal. So it makes sense for parents in those contexts to be called *abawayn*, following the patriarch or *ab* of the household in such matters.

I love how the Qur'an is so precise and how it is able to encapsulate both God's esteem and high regard for mothers and their lofty role of birth-givers, as well as of fathers and their patriarchal position. I love how even the Arabic word for womb 'raḥem' shares the same root as the word for divine mercy 'raḥma'! It is no accident that even people who do not believe in a supreme deity still refer to the creative, life-giving force in the world as 'Mother' Nature. Isn't it fascinating to know that the act of carrying and bringing new life into this world is what elicits God's mercy and forgiveness – not just on the mother, but on both parents? Simply examining the language and wording that He chooses to make his points helps me understand that God takes any opportunity to shower us parents with His blessings. And that no effort on our part is overlooked. His mercy truly permeates everything!

رَبَّنَا اغْفِرْ لِي وَلِوَالِدَيَّ وَلِلْمُؤْمِنِينَ يَوْمَ يَقُومُ الْحِسَابُ.

Our Lord! Forgive me, my parents and the believers on the Day the account is established.

(Sūra Ibrāhīm 14:41 - Prophet Ibrahim's supplication)

⁂ **Allah is so precise and eloquent with His wording, and tells us to use 'kind' words with our parents. What novel and kindly terms of endearment can you come up with for your parents and/or children to express your love and *raḥma* to them?**

⁂ **Have a go at composing your own supplication for your parents below:**

38. SLEEPING LIKE A BABY

وَجَعَلْنَا نَوْمَكُمْ سُبَاتًا.

And We have made your sleep a rest (for you).

(Sūra al-Naba' 78:9)

When I became a mother for the first time, bringing up a tiny baby abroad, away from friends, family and limited access to reading material or the internet, I was under the completely and gullible impression that babies loved sleeping! How far this was from the reality and how naïve, for my baby did not like to sleep one bit. He would protest at being put down for a nap, anxious that he was missing out on the world and all it had to offer him. He woke up several times in the night, and needed to be fed or rocked to sleep. Even when fast asleep in my arms, the very slightest movement or noise would startle him awake, and the whole routine of rocking him back to sleep had to be resumed. I became an expert rocker and mastered all the different ways to rock a baby: balancing him on outstretched legs and swaying side to side, bobbing him up and down while pacing the corridors, spreading him across my lap and rocking up and down, then like a rugby ball under my arm backwards and forwards, then side to side… You name it, I did it; but that boy did not stay asleep for more than a couple of hours at a time.

As he grew heavier and heavier, and I, more and more exhausted with lower back issues, I became a sleep-deprived zombie at my wits' end on how to get this kid to stay asleep at night. His average when not ill, teething, cold or gassy - was eight wakings a night, and it would take me up to an hour sometimes to get him back to sleep. I had recited every *du'a* and verse in the book, sung every song and nasheed, and even spiked his milk with nutmeg and saffron to make him drowsy in my utter desperation! They say children copy whatever we model for them. I modelled nodding off and sleeping many many times in front of him, but not once did he follow my lead in that department!

Now several years, three sleepy children, and a lot of reading later, here are a few of the tips that eventually worked for us:

1) Sleep is natural and God has made it a source of rest as He says in the verse above. It overtakes us whether we like it or not if the environment is conducive to it. For a baby, that means full tummy, no stimulation a good hour before bed, a nice dim room, and no separation anxiety, which is what my son had a serious bout of!

2) Sleep begets sleep! I had thought that cutting out his daytime naps and keeping him awake during the day would tire him out enough to want to go to bed. But it actually had the opposite effect. Illogical as it seemed, naps are biologically conducive to babies sleeping well at night!

3) Night-time must be differentiated from daytime. God makes mention of this many times in the Qur'an, speaking about the alternation of night and day, and their very different functions. He says, 'And He it is Who made for you the night that you might rest in it, and the day giving light; most surely there are signs in this for a people who would hear.'(Sūra Yūnus 10:67). Sleep experts and parenting books have entire chapters devoted to 'good sleep hygiene' - the technical term for winding down before bed and having a good bedtime routine.

4) Have realistic expectations. Sleeping through the night for babies does not mean 7am to 7pm, as some books claim. Their little tummies get hungry so their full nights look more like 12am to 5am. In expecting my baby to sleep through the entire night, I was setting myself up for failure.

5) Relax! I know from experience that this is far easier said than done, but now in hindsight, my own anxiety and frustration probably rubbed off on my son. I remember getting frustrated when as a toddler, he would drowsily ask for 'Five more minutes, Mummy?' when I had already spent the whole day with him, and the best part of the last hour trying to get him to sleep. I would sigh, plotting my next move, thinking resentfully of all the things still waiting to be done downstairs. Little did I know then, that by age 7, he would be asking for five more minutes in the park with his friends; by age 12, five more minutes on the Playstation; and now at age 15, five more minutes of sleep, because he simply can't seem to get enough of the stuff! And I'm sure there will come a time, when he will go off as an adult to university, and I will be the one craving for five more minutes with my son. Relax and get some perspective, this too shall pass!

6) I had read books advocating the let-them-cry-themselves-to-sleep method, and even went as far as trying it, again in my desperation. But it was painful to hear him cry! I felt a tightening in my chest, tears pricking my own eyes, my heart pounding inside my mouth, wishing I could just pick him up and take away his distress. Babies' cries do not just affect a mother's brain in a way that can be rationalised and justified, but pierce far deeper. Her entire body has been designed by God to react to his cries involuntarily: her heart aches, her breasts leak, her pulse races, her hands tingle and become sweaty, her head throbs and she feels distressed too. Call me a wimp, but to me in that moment, it simply felt wrong. I could not explain or justify it but his cry was like an alarm, and I just had to pick him up.

Later when my daughters were born and I was a little wiser, I learned that there is a big difference between a whinge before bed and a full-on bellowing cry. I had never let my son whinge or whimper, picking him up at the slightest 'eh', I had in fact spoiled him from Day One, so now he didn't know how to whinge without his mum coming to his rescue. With my daughters, I learned from Day One to let them settle to sleep with a few moans and groans here and there, even a loud wail of protest, without rushing to pick them up straight away, and to my surprise and delight, they soon learned to fall asleep all by themselves.

7) There is no quick fix to anything. The *ayahs* and *du'as* that are recommended to read to help babies sleep most definitely helped, but nothing works overnight. In the end it took a gentle, consistent approach of trying a combination of the above strategies, where I ultimately chose time over tears. Either way I was having to put in the time: hours in futile night wakings, or a little extra time with him consciously and lovingly before bed, reading to him, relaxing him, and dealing with his separation anxiety. In my case, time certainly trumped tears.

اللَّهُ لَا إِلَٰهَ إِلَّا هُوَ الْحَيُّ الْقَيُّومُ ۚ لَا تَأْخُذُهُ سِنَةٌ وَلَا نَوْمٌ ۚ لَّهُ مَا فِي السَّمَاوَاتِ وَمَا فِي الْأَرْضِ ۗ مَن ذَا الَّذِي يَشْفَعُ عِندَهُ إِلَّا بِإِذْنِهِ ۚ يَعْلَمُ مَا بَيْنَ أَيْدِيهِمْ وَمَا خَلْفَهُمْ ۖ وَلَا يُحِيطُونَ بِشَيْءٍ مِّنْ عِلْمِهِ إِلَّا بِمَا شَاءَ ۚ وَسِعَ كُرْسِيُّهُ السَّمَاوَاتِ وَالْأَرْضَ ۖ وَلَا يَئُودُهُ حِفْظُهُمَا ۚ وَهُوَ الْعَلِيُّ الْعَظِيمُ.

Allah - there is no god except Him - is the Living One, the all-Sustainer. Neither drowsiness befalls Him nor sleep. To Him belongs whatever is in the heavens and whatever is on the earth. Who is it that may intercede with Him except with His permission? He knows what is before them and what is behind them, and they do not comprehend anything of His knowledge except what He wishes. His seat embraces the heavens and the earth and He is not wearied by their preservation, and He is the all-Exalted, the all-Supreme.

(Sūra al-Baqara 2:255 - Ayat al-Kursi, the Verse of the Throne, which the Prophet (pbuh) is reported to have recited before bed)

- ✎ Did you have to deal with sleep issues with your baby or toddler?

- ✎ What were some of the strategies that worked for you and your family?

- ✎ What would you do differently now?

---

39. CUT THEM SOME SLACK

يَا أَيُّهَا الَّذِينَ آمَنُوا اجْتَنِبُوا كَثِيرًا مِّنَ الظَّنِّ إِنَّ بَعْضَ الظَّنِّ إِثْمٌ...

O you who believe! Avoid making too many assumptions – some assumptions are sinful…

(Sūra al-Ḥujurāt 49:12)

My daughter slumped next to me on the park bench, too tired to play anymore, as her siblings and cousins continued. 'Go and play!' I urged her. She said she just wanted to sit for a while and watch them play. As we sat, watching all the children in the playground with their parents, taking in all the hubbub of that blustery autumn Sunday morning, I noticed a man glued to his phone screen as his child played nearby, calling out: 'Daddy, Daddy, watch me!' Gosh, I thought to myself, what's the point of coming to the park and being stuck on your phone? What could be more delightful and important than watching your child play? A boy ran past us wearing nothing but shorts and a t-shirt - surely he would catch a cold in this weather, I remarked to myself. What kind of parents let their child out dressed that way in such cold weather? A woman nearby looked visibly frazzled as she tried to calm her three children all having tantrums near an ice cream van. Clearly, she had said no, but was still hanging around while they watched others getting ice creams! She should just walk away and stop trying to negotiate with them, I thought to myself.

Judgments like these pass through our minds effortlessly every day as we assume we would do a much better job parenting other people's children as we have so perfectly done with our own! As ridiculous as this sounds, that is exactly what I was doing in that moment as I made assumptions about each of those parents in my mind. Granted, I did not voice them out loud to my daughter, and they may have been true, but I had no business passing any judgment on anybody's parenting when I had several flaws of my own. I clearly was not delighting in watching my children play in that moment either!

From our own vantage points on the bench, it seems so easy to judge a situation or a person out in the field, but we have no idea about their lives, their principles, their choices or their children. They say that it is often those who have no children who pass the harshest judgments on parents and their children at the supermarket checkout. Until they become parents themselves! Unfortunately, even when we do become parents, we are reluctant to cut fellow parents some slack. Prophet Isa (pbuh) said, *'How can you notice a speck in your brother's eye but overlook the plank in your own?!'* We all too often make judgments about other children's behaviour or how their parents discipline them, imagining that we could do a better job ourselves: 'If he were my son...' 'I would have...' 'She should definitely...', but these are unfair judgments, without any real information or understanding of their circumstances, and lacking in compassion. Our judgments, though often well-meaning, can also be fuelled by pride or self-righteousness. God warns us about making too many assumptions in the verse above, and even goes as far as to say that it is a sin.

It is not that we should never make judgments, or that there aren't right and wrong ways to do things - of course there are. But we tend to notice other people's shortcomings whilst oblivious to our own. They say mistakes are the easiest and most difficult: easiest to notice in others and most difficult to notice in ourselves. And God forbid passing judgment or making assumptions should make us feel any better about ourselves! We never know how far someone has come, and we can never know what a family is going through. As parents, we need to be careful of thinking that the way we do things is the *only* right way to do things.

Sadly, our assumptions can escalate into full blown judgments about someone and how they are *as a person*. When we go to a fellow mother's house and find it disorganised, it does not mean she is disorganised and messy all of the time. If we see her nervous or worried about something one day, it does not mean that she is a nervous wreck all of the time. If we see her feeding her children cereal for dinner one day, it does not mean that she does that every day of the week, or can't cook or that her children are malnourished. If we see her lose her temper with a child testing her last nerve, it does not automatically mean she is an angry and out-of-control parent. Most of us parents would be in serious trouble if the same stringent yardsticks were used to judge us.

Children are not plants or inanimate objects, and their trajectory of growth and development definitely does not follow a straight line. They come with no instruction manual, often disappoint us, and are certainly not perfect. If yours are and you feel pleased with how they have turned out, then praise God, not yourself. Do not take the credit. Never feel superior to another parent because they are fighting a battle you know nothing about. It is not tasteful to jump in to give advice to other parents about their children unless it is expressly asked of us. If He has given you an easier time in parenting, then it is not because of your awesomeness or that you deserve it, but because He is infinitely Generous.

Of course, at times, our observations are merely that: observations. Not assumptions or judgments, and we genuinely feel care or concern towards another parent, visibly having a hard time. Besides praying for them, we would love to be able to extend the hand of grace, offer help or support, but that is not always easy to do, because again, as well-meaning as our intentions are, we in turn feel like we will be judged as busy-bodies or self-righteous parents who think they know better. I know I have often held back from offering to help a struggling mother because of not wanting to come across as patronising. So what is one to do? How to express compassion and solidarity without making the parent feel less than?

There's a phrase that a kind lady once used with me when I was visibly struggling whilst travelling with my three young children on an aeroplane, and she offered to help me. As I looked at her apologetically, embarrassed and frazzled at the clumsy mess and clatter my children were making with their lunch trays, she said, 'It's okay - I'm a mother too'. That short phrase and the way that it made me feel in that moment struck relief in me and stuck with me thereafter. I did not feel judged or patronised, but instead felt like she understood what I was going through. I was able to accept her help gratefully, without apologising or feeling embarrassed.

At that moment in the park, I had to remind myself that every parent was going through his or her own struggle that I knew nothing about, just like me. And like the lady on the plane, if ever I wanted to step in and help out, and it was appropriate to do so, all I had to do was say, 'It's okay - I'm a mother too'.

وَأَجْرِ لِلنَّاسِ عَلَى يَدَيَّ الْخَيْرَ، وَلَا تَمْحَقْهُ بِالْمَنِّ وَهَبْ لِي مَعَالِيَ الأَخْلَاقِ، وَاعْصِمْنِي مِنَ الْفَخْرِ....

Let good flow out from my hands towards people and efface it not by my making them feel obliged! Give me the highest moral traits and preserve me from pride…

(Extract from Imam Zayn al-Abidin's Du'a Makārim al-Akhlāq - his Supplication for Noble Moral Traits no. 20 in Sahifa al-Sajjadiyya)

>>> What prompts you to make judgments about someone else's parenting?

>>> How has God used motherhood to make you more humble?

>>> What are some specific ways that you could show greater compassion to other mums?

40. GRIEVING A BABY

اللَّـهُ يَعْلَمُ مَا تَحْمِلُ كُلُّ أُنْثَىٰ وَمَا تَغِيضُ الْأَرْحَامُ وَمَا تَزْدَادُ ۖ وَكُلُّ
شَيْءٍ عِندَهُ بِمِقْدَارٍ ﴿٨﴾
عَالِمُ الْغَيْبِ وَالشَّهَادَةِ الْكَبِيرُ الْمُتَعَالِ ﴿٩﴾

Allah knows what every female carries [in her womb], and by how much the wombs fall short and exceed; and everything with Him is in [precise measure]. The Knower of the seen and the Unseen, the All-great, the All-sublime.

(Sūra al-Ra'd 13:8-9)

To the mother who has recently lost her baby - be it through miscarriage, as a stillborn babe, or held him for a mere few moments then had to say goodbye -: Allah knows.

Allah knows that your heartbreak is as real and excruciating as any physical pain, and that the loss of a child is one of the greatest trials to befall a human being. His own beloved Messenger was tried with the same, and he too mourned his infant son. The best woman ever created, Lady Fatima (pbuh), suffered no less trauma.

Allah knows the emotional anguish you are going through: of never holding the baby you grew so attached to in your womb, never meeting her or watching her personality unfold and never getting to shower her with your uncontainable love. He knows how much you wanted her, the joy that flooded your heart and made it flutter every time the realization of your pregnancy hit you anew; and the mark that her short time in this world will leave on that soft heart of yours.

Allah knows the anxieties and worries that plague your mind, as irrational and unfounded as they may be: What if I don't conceive again? What if I did something to cause this? What if I never recover from this? Is there something wrong with me?

Allah knows your need for space, your need to grieve and mourn. He knows that for you, right now, the pain is as real as having lost an existing child. He knows when you have no will to articulate your grief to others, or to explain anything to anyone, and He also knows when you need to talk about it incessantly just to feel less numb.

Allah knows your deepest fears, whether it is your first child or your fourth. He knows a mother's heart and that to her, every baby is precious. To him too, every soul that He has created is precious and counted, and so is your baby.

Allah knows the pain you are going through - of engorged breasts and leaking milk - at the mere thought of nursing your baby. He sees the physical pain you are experiencing, and He does not let anything go unrecompensed, for He says '... I will not waste the work of any worker among you, whether male or female...' (Sūra Āl ʿImrān 3:195). He knows how much you can endure and what is too much to bear, and He has promised that He will never burden anyone with more than their capacity to bear. He knows you are strong enough.

Allah knows that you have it in you to surmount this, even though you may not think so right now. Your heart may feel as if it will never heal from this gaping wound, but take heart: He is the Great Physician who gently and discreetly heals physical gashes as well as emotional wounds, leaving only a scar where the wound once was, as a reminder of where you have been on your journey, and how, by His Grace, you have healed and grown stronger and even more beautiful.

Allah knows you are broken at this moment, but He has a special use for broken things: broken clouds pour rain, broken soil yields crops, broken seeds give growth to new shoots, broken wheat produces bread, and broken hearts let in His light through the cracks.

Allah knows His own plans. Your little bundle is part and parcel of His precise system and meticulous plan. The Prophet said he would proudly count miscarried and stillborn babies as part of his *ummah*. Allah's decree was for you not to have what was not meant for you at this time, but if He can take away something you never imagined losing, then surely he can grant you something you never imagined gaining, for in His Hands is only good. And soon, He will show you the good in this too, that you may witness His wise ways and say: *Alḥamdulillāh, We all belong to Him and to Him we are all returning (sooner or later) (innā lillāhi wa innā ilayhi rāji'ūn).*

Allah knows best.

رَبِّ هَبْ لِي مِنَ الصَّالِحِينَ

My Lord, grant me [a child] from the righteous ones.

(Sūra al-Ṣāffāt 37:100 - Prophet Ibrahim's du'a for a child)

رَبِّ هَبْ لِي مِن لَّدُنكَ ذُرِّيَّةً طَيِّبَةً ۖ إِنَّكَ سَمِيعُ الدُّعَاءِ

My Lord, grant me from Yourself goodly offspring;
indeed You are the Hearer of supplications.

رَبِّ لَا تَذَرْنِي فَرْدًا وَأَنتَ خَيْرُ الْوَارِثِينَ.

My Lord, do not leave me without an heir,
and You are the best of inheritors.

(Sūra Āl 'Imrān 3:38 and Sūra Anbiyā' 21:89 -
Prophet Zakariyya's du'as for a child)

41. THE BEST INVISIBLE FRIEND

لاَ أُقْسِمُ بِالنَّفْسِ اللَّوَّامَة

"Nay! I swear by the self-reproaching soul!"

(Sūra al-Qiyāma 75:2)

Tatiyana was her name - my daughter's invisible friend, when she was around five years old, who she could happily chat away to and play with when there was no one else around to listen to all her babbling. After having watched the friendship between her favourite cartoon character, Lola, and her imaginary friend, Soren Lorenson, my daughter had decided that she too needed her own invisible friend. Thankfully, she didn't use Tatiyana as a scapegoat for all her naughty antics half as much as Lola blamed Soren Lorenson for hers!

Friends are mentioned by Allah in the Qur'an quite a few times, but with many different names. There are at least seven types of friends mentioned in the Qur'an, and they each differ slightly in their friendship, closeness and affinity. God uses the word *walī*, for example, to refer to a protective friend who always looks out for your best interests. They may even be older than you in a mentor-type of relationship, and always have your back. Imam Ali (pbuh) is often referred to as 'Walī Allah' - the protective friend of God - because of his protectiveness over Islam and the Muslims. Allah calls Himself the Walī of the believers - their protective friend - and those who take Allah as their *walī* have no cause to fear anything nor to grieve as they are convinced of His special protection, as in the verse, 'Now surely the friends of Allah - they shall have no fear nor shall they grieve.' (Sūra Yūnus 10:62).

He uses the word *khalīl* for a very intimate friend, usually around common interests, who enjoy each other's company. Allah says that He takes Prophet Ibrahim (pbuh) as His *khalīl* since Ibrahim ran to Him with every little thing and followed Him to the letter. Allah, in turn, entrusted him with building the Ka'ba. However, Allah also warns us against taking the wrong type of *khalīl* for a friend. He says that on the Day of Judgment, people will deeply regret whom they took as a *khalīl*, biting their hands in remorse, saying, 'Oh how I wish I had taken a path with the Prophet! How ruined I am! How I wish I had not taken so and so for a friend!' (Sūra al-Furqān 25:27-28). We are being warned against the types of friendships that lead us astray, of following the wrong types of friends for whom we bend our principles in our bid to impress them or keep up with them. The sad thing is that we won't even remember their names, for Allah says '*so and so*', meaning that these so called 'friends' that we followed, obsessed over, 'stalked' on Instagram, knowing everything there was to know about them, probably did not even know we existed, but inadvertently led us astray.

One of my personal favourite words for friend that Allah mentions is *rafīq*, because its root denotes comfort and relaxation. The word cushion or pillow in Arabic, *mirfaq*, comes from the same root. A *rafīq*, therefore, is a friend you can lean on; someone that you can chill out and relax with; someone around whom you can be completely yourself. Allah describes the best types of *rafīqs* that one can have: 'And whoever obeys Allah and the Messenger, these are those upon whom Allah has bestowed favours from among the prophets, the truthful ones, the martyrs and the righteous ones, and what great company they are!' (Sūra al-Nisā' 4:69). Imagine having that kind of comfortable and relaxed camaraderie with the Prophet himself! Needless to say, that will only be possible if we harbour the same kind of love and attachment to him in this life, and feel at ease with his sayings and teachings right here.

A very special friend that Allah mentions, and even swears by, to make His point in the Qur'an, is one that we cannot physically see and often neglect to even acknowledge her existence in the verse, 'Nay! I swear by the self-reproaching soul.' (Sūra al-Qiyāma 75:2). Her name is *nafs al-lawwāma*, (the self-reproaching soul), who we can refer to as our inner Jiminy Cricket, our conscience. Unfortunately, we often refer to her in negative terms as: the 'guilty' conscience, or my conscience 'bit' me, or is 'gnawing' at me, or my conscience 'won't let me sleep'. True, we often try to avoid this annoying friend of ours though she has actually been designed to stop us from doing wrong things. And she does this by getting our attention, in whatever way she can: through the knot in our stomachs, the racing pulse, the sweaty palms, the replaying of words we wish we hadn't said - all to make us aware of what we have done wrong so that we can make amends and ask for forgiveness.

Unfortunately, we ignore her and shut her voice out. Guilt is perceived as a bad thing. 'Take it out of your mind', they say. 'Don't carry guilt around. Let it go'. But she does not let up easily. Interestingly, in Arabic, her very name: *lawwāma* has an air of persistence about it. The Arabic language has fascinating patterns that lend specific meanings to words based on what they sound like, so all words that follow the same sound pattern will carry a similar connotation. So, a *ghassāl* is someone who washes clothes every day as a profession, a *khabbāz* is a baker who bakes every day, a *sajjād* is one who prostrates regularly. Allah is *ghaffār* and *tawwāb* because He forgives and pardons our sins constantly. Can you hear the sound pattern? So our old friend, *lawwāma*, is called the self-reproaching soul precisely because of her constant badgering us and not giving up on us. That is her job. And although invisible, she is not imaginary at all, but is a very real gift from Allah: our internal alarm in precarious situations. The more we heed her voice, the louder it gets, and the stronger the relationship develops until her voice turns from guilt after the misdeed to a gut feeling stopping us in our tracks before a misdeed.

As we become aware of our *nafs al-lawwāma*, it may not be a bad idea to introduce our children to their own invisible best friend and to teach them to listen to her voice deep inside.

اللّهُمَّ آتِ نَفْسِيْ تَقْوَاهَا وَزَكِّها أَنْتَ خَيْرُ مَنْ زَكَّاهَا.
أَنْتَ وَلِيُّهَا وَمَوْلَاهَا.

O Allah! Grant my soul its protection and piety, and purify it for You are the best one to purify it. You are its friend and its patron.

(Supplication recommended for the strengthening and purification of the soul)

➤ **Can you think of times in your life when your *nafs al-lawwāma* has tried to grab your attention and stop you from a potentially harmful situation?**

➤ **What happened when you either heeded or ignored her voice?**

42. GO AND PRAY!

وَأْمُرْ أَهْلَكَ بِالصَّلَاةِ وَاصْطَبِرْ عَلَيْهَا ۖ لَا نَسْأَلُكَ رِزْقًا ۖ نَّحْنُ نَرْزُقُكَ ۗ وَالْعَاقِبَةُ لِلتَّقْوَىٰ.

And bid your family to prayer and be steadfast in maintaining it. We do not ask any provision of you: it is We who provide for you, and to Godwariness belongs the ultimate outcome [in the Hereafter].

(Sūra Ṭā Hā 20:132)

The questions that parents most often ask of scholars, in one form or another, are: 'How do I get my children to pray?' 'My kids are averse to praying, what can I do?' 'Getting my kids to pray, especially *fajr*, is always such a struggle! Help!' 'Is there a special *du'a* I can recite to make my children pray?' Take heart. Apart from a few lucky parents, most of us find ourselves in that boat at some point or another along our parenting journey, and the very fact that God has emphasised for us as parents to bid our children to pray in the above verse makes it an even heavier responsibility to bear. But perhaps it is precisely our view of *salat* as a burden or *taklif* is where the problem lies. My teacher always used to say, 'If children are not enjoying *salat* or doing it begrudgingly, then it is because we as teachers or parents have failed to introduce it to them properly." It's true that *salat* gets a bad rep from our very mouths when we say things like:

'At least *salat* is over and done with. '

'I forgot I still have to pray.'

'I'm so tired... I so can't be bothered to pray right now.'

'Yessss, I don't have to pray today.'

'It's okay, there's still some time before it gets *qadha*.'

'*Salat* would be so much easier if we didn't have to remove everything to do *wudhu* first.'

Admittedly, I have been guilty of some of these in the past, and now have to be extra careful not to use the same language to refer to *salat*, especially around young impressionable hearts and minds. Before we can bid our children to pray, it is so important for us to shift our mindset from seeing it as something we 'have' to do, to an opportunity to converse with our Lord; as a way to recharge ourselves and plug into our Power Source; as our souls' nourishment that we look forward to as much as we look forward to eating. Above all, our children need to *see* us look forward to prayer time, dropping everything to go and pray, enjoying it, taking our time with it, and not seeing it as a chore. Below is a collection of 10 practical tips that have worked for me and fellow parents in instilling a love and habit of prayer in our children over the years, in no particular order of importance:

1) Starting young. Even before the formal age of introducing the actions of the prayer or the recitations, it's important to allow them to hear us actually conversing with Allah in English or whatever their mother tongue is. The best time to do this is to either invite them onto our prayer mats straight after we've finished so we can raise our hands and talk to Allah together, or as we spend quality time with them before bed. Ask them, 'What would you like to pray about?' Their cuteness in asking for random things will bowl you over, but give them the freedom to pour out their hearts.

2) Getting them their own prayer mat on a special occasion, with their own little perfume, *tasbih*, and prayer clothes, that they cherish and look after.

3) Not letting praying in their own rooms become a habit. Communal prayer has been emphasised far more than praying individually, and it's important that they see prayer as a family activity, even if it is not a formal congregational prayer with an *imam*. I have found that my own children love leading the prayer, and love the sound of their own voices reciting, even if they do not like to recite in public otherwise. Having a rotating *salat* monitor in charge of noting *salat* time each day and reciting *adhan*, another in charge of laying out the prayer mats, another in charge of leading, etc… can go a long way towards making it a family practice as ingrained as having dinner together. Afterwards, everyone hugs each other, and they come to associate *salat* with affection and family cohesion. When my teens are reluctant to pray together so they can rush off to do their homework, it helps to gently remind them that a family who prays together stays together, and that it is my favourite part of the day.

4) Children find it hard to focus, and maintain concentration throughout the prayer, as do even most adults! Again, when they show reluctance, asking why they have to pray anyway, and moaning about how it's so boring, it is better not to shut them down and force them, but instead to gently keep reminding them of the benefits of praying. We can teach them about *salat* being a force-field or 'shield against wrongdoing and indecency' (Sūra ʿAnkabūt 29:45), or food for the soul. I remember my daughter once remarking that at least if we could see its effects on the soul, it would be easier to do, but since we can't see or feel what it even does, it's hard to maintain. Upon hearing that, my son piped up and said, 'Well it's just like a treadmill that the fat person needs to go on. He doesn't want to because he doesn't see results straight away, but when he keeps at it for a long time, then he will see results, just like mummy and how she loves *salat* now that she's been praying for long enough!' I guess that's one way of putting it! If witnessing the effects of *salat* is important to them, then we can show them that we are more relaxed parents after *salat*, smile at them, hug them and let them see a change in our demeanour.

5) It also helps to verbalise our intentions out loud, and to say, in English or whatever our most comfortable language is: I am praying *maghrib* to connect with God, and right now there is nowhere else I'd rather be.'

6) Refraining from barking orders: 'Go and pray first!' 'Have you prayed yet?' 'Why have you still not prayed?' This is a habit that I have found so difficult to break, as my children say I'm obsessed with getting them to pray. From experience, though, the best policy has been to just start praying myself, so that they come and follow suit. Nagging for *salat* only has the opposite effect as it becomes yet one more thing that they become parent-deaf to. It's also important to give them the onus of being mindful of their own *salat*, as with other things that they become responsible for as they grow older.

Instead of always asking, 'Have you prayed?', we can ask instead: '*How* was your *salat*?' which gives them the space to think about the quality of their *salat*. God too asks us in the Qur'an: '*How are you acting?*' (Sūra Yūnus 10:14). And it's an important question designed to make us think about the quality of our actions. And encourage them to answer honestly, by expressing the honest truth about your own *salat*: I think I rushed it a bit today… It was ok… It could have been better... It was great... I feel so much more at peace now... Gosh I really needed that... I really tried to concentrate today, and so on, so that they understand that it is not a tick-box exercise, but rather something to aspire towards practicing and perfecting, and something they need to be mindful in.

7) Allowing them to meet their physical needs first after school. It's okay to let them have a quick snack and freshen up, unless time is running out. To tell them that they can't eat until they have prayed only makes them resent *salat* and rush it unnecessarily.

8) Making sure that they see us revolving our day around it, even when we are making plans to go out: before *zuhr*, after *maghrib*, where will we pray,… so they can see where our priorities are.

9) Schools are increasingly incorporating mindfulness techniques and yoga in classrooms. We can link the two together and show our children how Allah has already taught us these techniques and stances in stillness, meditation and mindfulness long ago, that people are only just discovering the benefits of.

10) Teaching them by the Prophet and the Ahl al-Bayt's (pbuh) examples: that he loved to pray so much that he said that *salat* was the coolness of his eye. His companions reported that when it was time for prayer, it was as if he recognised no one. Our Imams took even the physical postures in *salat* very seriously, and perfected them to such an extent that they were often described as being as straight as arrows, because they did not fidget or rush. In the same vein, we must ensure that we commend our children regularly on their beautiful actions, their sweet voices, and their timely adherence to *salat*. Imam Husayn (pbuh) blessed and prayed for his companion who remembered *salat* in the midst of the battle on the Day of Ashura. Little anecdotes like that and praising our children in turn go a long way towards instilling love for *salat* in their hearts.

رَبِّ اجْعَلْنِي مُقِيمَ الصَّلَاةِ وَمِن ذُرِّيَّتِي ۚ رَبَّنَا وَتَقَبَّلْ دُعَاءِ.

My Lord! Make me one who upholds the prayer and my descendants [as well]; and our Lord, accept my supplication.

(Sūra Ibrahim 14:40 - Prophet Ibrahim (pbuh)'s supplication for himself and his children)

꙳ What are some of the challenges you face in bidding your children to pray, or in feeling motivated to pray yourself?

꙳ How have you managed to overcome those challenges?

꙳ Try asking yourself, and even your children, after each *salat* today, *"How was your salat?"*

---

43. SHAKOOR

وَقَلِيلٌ مِّنْ عِبَادِيَ الشَّكُورُ.

*But very few of My servants are **shakoor**.*

(Sūra Saba' 34:13)

If there was one quality or adjective I would love to be called by God besides a believer, it would be "*Shakoor*". The *Shakoor* ones are those in His inner circle, those whom there are very few of among God's servants - by His own assertion above -, and a name that He has reserved for only a select handful of people in the Qur'an, namely the likes of heroes like Prophet Nuh (pbuh), in the verse: 'Surely he (Nuh) was a *shakoor* servant.' (Sūra al-Isrā' 17:3). Yes, yes, I know: wishful thinking on my part! I have a very very long way to go before anybody is going to call me that name, but I can certainly aspire!

So, what does *Shakoor* mean? Obsessively and actively grateful. The fact that Allah states many times over that very few of His servants are obsessively grateful should make us want to be in the inner circle even more! And the fact that Shaytan also pipes up and says to God, 'You will not find most of them to be grateful' (Sūra al-A'rāf 7:17), should make us even more determined to be counted in this special category of people.

Interestingly, *Shakoor* is also a name that God calls Himself: 'He will pay them their dues and increase them of His grace. Indeed, He is most-Forgiving, most-Appreciative.' (Sūra al-Fāṭir 35:30). He describes Himself as One who appreciates His servants' efforts at drawing near to Him, with their striving and hard work; 'Whoever desires the hereafter and strives for it as he ought to strive, being a believer, then as for those, their striving shall surely be appreciated' (Sūra al-Isrā' 17:19). What a wonderful God we have, Who firstly appreciates our striving, then reserves its fruits solely for us to benefit from; 'Whoever is grateful is grateful only for his own sake' (Sūra al-Naml 27:40), then rewards us abundantly just for being grateful for His bounties, and then increases our capacity to receive yet more gifts from Him; 'And when your Lord announced: If you are grateful, I will certainly increase you...' (Sūra Ibrahim 14:7).

In addition to all that, He outlines to us exactly what we are to be grateful for, so that we are not left with any doubt or excuse. He reminds us, in various places in the Qur'an, to be grateful for:

- His guidance
- His help and victory, and averting many dangers from us
- His overlooking our numerous mistakes
- His provision and food
- His providing us with fresh - and not salty - water to drink
- His purification and provision of pure water for us to cleanse ourselves with
- His making the earth subservient to us as a means of security and provision
- His making the sea subservient to us for transportation, seafood and pearls
- His grace and kindness at every turn
- Making cattle subservient to us for their meat, milk and hides
- His provision of fruits of all different varieties
- Breathing of His Own Spirit into us and perfecting our creation
- Alternation of night and day so that we may work and rest

- Dispatching of winds to bring rain to all corners of the earth

- His gifting us with all our senses: sight, hearing, reasoning

- and many more.

The Prophet's family (pbut) too have taught us many lessons in expressing gratitude through the multitude of their sayings and supplications. I marvel at Imam Husayn (pbuh)'s gratitude list in his *Du'a 'Arafa*, with detailed thanks for seemingly insignificant things like the webbing between his fingers, the ridges in his palette and the lines on his forehead amidst surrendering that we would never be able to enumerate all His blessings. Imam Zayn al-'Abidīn (pbuh) too, has composed a very beautiful supplication titled *Munājāt al-Shākirīn*, the Whispered Conversation of the Grateful Ones, where he goes as far as to thank Allah for the very ability to thank him! They teach us how to eloquently include 'thank you' and 'I love you' in our *du'as*, and not just 'I need' and 'I want'.

As far as gratitude goes, I'd say that after my life, my faith and my health, I am very grateful for my children, as I am sure you are too. We often refer to them as blessings and gifts from God, and thank Him regularly for them. We thank Him for keeping them safe and healthy, for keeping them on the straight path and for the joy that they bring to us. Interestingly though, they do not seem to feature explicitly in the Qur'an as something we are urged to be expressly grateful for the way that God has outlined other things. Perhaps it is because Allah, in His infinite wisdom, knows that gratefulness for those that we are besotted with and invested in anyway, comes quite naturally to us. Perhaps His list encompasses precisely those things that we neglect to appreciate and often take for granted. Such as our parents.

Parents are a separate category that Allah has reserved special mention for in the department of gratitude. He not only tells us to be grateful *for* them, but also to express our gratitude *to* them. He says, 'Be grateful to Me and to both your parents' (Sūra Luqmān 31:14). Not only that, but in the same verse, He outlines exactly *why* we need to express our gratitude to them: 'His mother bore him with great strain upon strain, and his weaning took two years...' It is quite remarkable that for the natural act of childbearing, delivery and weaning that our mothers undertook, both parents become deserving of our thanks. He makes no mention of all the other things that they have done for us and continue to do: clothing, sheltering, protecting, nurturing, educating, and then babysitting our children on top of that! That means that whether they are Muslim or not, good-doers or not, did a good job of raising us or not – we still owe them true thanks for the simple fact that our mothers laboured in carrying, birthing and weaning us. He even teaches us how to articulate that thanks to Him, and pray for them, and to serve them in their old age and weakness as they looked after us in our time of weakness. In His kindness, He has spelled out exactly what we need to do to become worthy of that special title "Shakoor": obsessively and actively be grateful to Him, and to our parents.

رَبِّ أَوْزِعْنِي أَنْ أَشْكُرَ نِعْمَتَكَ الَّتِي أَنْعَمْتَ عَلَيَّ وَعَلَىٰ وَالِدَيَّ وَأَنْ أَعْمَلَ صَالِحًا تَرْضَاهُ وَأَصْلِحْ لِي فِي ذُرِّيَّتِي ۖ إِنِّي تُبْتُ إِلَيْكَ وَإِنِّي مِنَ الْمُسْلِمِينَ.

My Lord! Inspire me to give thanks for Your blessing with which You have blessed me and my parents, and that I may do righteous deeds which please You, and invest my descendants with righteousness. Indeed, I have turned to you in penitence, and I am one of the Muslims.

(Sūra Aḥqāf 46:15)

✹ Make your own list of things that you are grateful for today.

✹ Gratitude in the Qur'an is not just a sentiment to be felt, but a behaviour to be expressed: how are you going to express your thanks to your parents, and what will you do today to show them that you truly appreciate them?

44. CHERISH HIS LITTLENESS

هُوَ الَّذِي خَلَقَكُم مِّن تُرَابٍ ثُمَّ مِن نُّطْفَةٍ ثُمَّ مِنْ عَلَقَةٍ ثُمَّ يُخْرِجُكُمْ
طِفْلًا ثُمَّ لِتَبْلُغُوا أَشُدَّكُمْ ثُمَّ لِتَكُونُوا شُيُوخًا
وَمِنكُم مَّن يُتَوَفَّىٰ مِن قَبْلُ ۚ وَلِتَبْلُغُوا أَجَلًا مُّسَمًّى وَلَعَلَّكُمْ تَعْقِلُونَ.

It is He who created you from dust, then from a drop of [seminal]
fluid, then from a clinging mass, then He brings you forth as infants,
then [He nurtures you] so that you may come of age, and then
that you may become aged—though there are some of you who die
earlier—and complete a specified term, and so that you may exercise
your reason.

(Sūra al-Ghāfir 40:67)

I have just come back from the hospital, utterly smitten with my newly arrived baby nephew. He is extra special because we have not had a baby in the family for the last ten years! As I held his sleepy, downy, little head against my chest, his tiny body fitting snuggly into my forearms, it took me back in time to when my own children - now all taller than me - were tiny babies themselves. And as his tiny fingers wrapped around mine, I wept, overwhelmed, as I stood there holding him. I wept tears of wonderment at how Allah had created his perfect little fingers and toes, and his dainty little features a perfect combination of his parents; I wept tears of having witnessed utter beauty in watching my little sister in her new role as a mother; I wept tears of joy at welcoming the new addition to our family; and I wept tears of longing for my own children as new-borns. How I missed them at this stage, now that it would never again return!

Time does not stand still for anyone, and as I have reflected back over the years, there have been many occasions when I wished time would just stand still and I could freeze my children in all their littleness, and enjoy them at each stage for just a bit longer: the stage when they would make all their funny faces, grimaces, smiles and frowns in their sleep and I would watch them, entranced. Or when as crawling babies, every peek-a-boo and every snap of a rubber band, or every popping sound made them burst into fits of giggles. Or when they were toddlers lunging forward, trying to jump and run before their chubby feet could even walk yet. Or when they were in pre-school, babbling away randomly, when I would make them repeat their adorably cute mispronunciation of words, just so I could hang onto their every syllable. Or when they asked 'Why' about everything, in their curious and wide-eyed wonderment about the world.

But it was that very littleness that also drove me crazy at times, making me wish that they would just hurry up and grow up faster, so they would stop waking up at night, sleep for longer in the mornings, be more independent, get out of nappies, feed themselves, stop whining and use words, give me some space, and go to school already. And now, here I am, regretting that I ever wished for them to grow up faster, and aching inside for that precious, fleeting littleness that vanishes far too quickly.

Bask in his littleness, I tell my sister, breathe in his powdery, milky scent of heaven, and soak in the sight of his stretching and yawning in all his newborn glory. Hold him tight and hold him close against your chest, feeling his little heartbeat against yours. Marvel at how quickly his body will grow in these next few months, but don't will him to grow up too fast. Enjoy your special, uninterrupted feedings at night, for as disruptive to your sleep as they may seem, leaving your eyes with dark circles, the sleepless nights that we have when they are teens are far more difficult to bear, and leave us with white hair. Enjoy these ones now and thank God for the opportunity. Cradle him and carry him as much as you want – there will come a time when he will try to use his little feet to run away from you and wriggle out of your arms at every opportunity he gets. Stare at him and absorb the sight of him; imprint it in your mind at every stage, for no camera can capture the beauty that a mother's eye can see in her children's faces. Breathe in his fragrant baby scent and his sweet breath, fresh out of new lungs, as you cuddle his little, warm body against yours, for even as exciting as each new stage and new milestone is, this littleness of his shall pass in the blink of an eye.

As I come home to my children and look at them afresh with dewy eyes, I see them in their 'teenage' littleness, for compared to adulthood tomorrow, today they are still my babies, and still little. And I promise myself to cherish their littleness today.

اَللّٰهُمَّ وَمُنَّ عَلَىَّ بِبَقَآءِ وُلْدِىْ وَبِاِصْلَاحِهِمْ لِىْ وَبِاِمْتَاعِىْ بِهِمْ

اِلٰهِىْ اُمْدُدْلِىْ فِىْ اَعْمَارِهِمْ وَزِدْلِىْ فِىْ اَجَالِهِمْ,

وَرَبِّ لِىْ صَغِيْرَهُمْ وَقَوِّ لِىْ ضَعِيْفَهُمْ وَاَصِحَّ لِىْ اَبْدَانَهُمْ وَأَدْيَانَهُمْ

وَاَخْلَاقَهُمْ. وَعَافِهِمْ فِىْ اَنْفُسِهِمْ وَفِىْ جَوَارِحِهِمْ

وَفِىْ كُلِّ مَا عُنِيْتُ بِهِ مِنْ اَمْرِهِمْ وَأَدْرِرْ لِىْ وَعَلٰى يَدَىَّ اَرْزَاقَهُمْ.

O Allah, be kind to me through the survival of my children setting them right for me, and allowing me to enjoy them!
My God! Make long their lives for me, increase their terms, bring up the smallest for me, strengthen the weakest for me, rectify for me their bodies, their religious dedication, and their moral traits, make them well in their souls, their limbs, and everything that concerns me of their affair, and pour out for me and upon my hand their provisions!

(Extract from Imam Zayn al-Abidin (pbuh)'s
Supplication for his Children no.25 from Sahifa al-Sajjadiyya)

197

⟫⌐ Looking back at your children as new-borns, what did you used to wish that you could 'freeze'?

⟫⌐ What are you going to cherish about their 'littleness' as they are today?

_____

_____

_____

_____

_____

_____

_____

_____

_____

_____

_____

45. BUT WHY?

وَقَالَ رَبُّكُمُ ادْعُونِي أَسْتَجِبْ لَكُمْ

Your Lord has said, 'Call Me, and I will respond to you!'

(Sūra al-Ghāfir 40:60)

My youngest daughter was an inquisitive little chatterbox from the moment she started talking. She wanted to know 'Why' about everything, 'How' it was all going to happen, and 'When' we were going to get there? She would want to know the reasons behind every little thing I did, such as why I was wearing this scarf and not that one, as well as big questions like why we couldn't see God, and why people who were as old as I was were not any taller! As exasperating as our children's incessant barrage of questions are sometimes, we know that this is a mark of their curiosity, their innocence, and their drive to discover the world around them. This is all part of their God-given, naturally in-built *fiṭra* (instinct) to want answers and search for meaning in this life, and we, as their parents, have the tough job of providing those answers, which in the beginning I found quite scary, and admittedly often blagged my way through. What I only realised later was that we don't have to know or provide all the answers, but encourage them to think for themselves and point them in the right direction to find the answers. So when I would tell her: 'Why don't you Google it?' or 'What do you think the answer to that is?' or 'Who do you think could help us answer that?', she would sigh and roll her eyes, clearly just wanting the easy answer from my mouth.

As an adult, I also find myself asking 'Why' a lot of the time, not overtly but deep down, and unlike my child, my questions are not directed to a knowledgeable person or to a parent, but to God Himself:

Why is this happening to me?

What do You want from me?

When will relief come?

Why are my prayers not being answered?

Why can't I just have a sign that this is the right choice?

Why has Islam got such rules in the first place?

Why do you not just intervene?

(and many more).

I ask Him my questions, and then I follow up with yet another one: 'Why can't I hear Your responses to me even though You have promised to respond to the caller when he calls You?' I, like my child, want the easy answer, but God in all His wisdom, has better ideas, though it takes some getting used to. My daughter is not the only impatient one!

God does not tire of our questions and encourages us to think about the answers ourselves. Like a wise parent, He does not blurt out the answer, but asks instead: 'What do you think the answer to that is?' Throughout the Qur'an, He asks us His own questions to make us think: *'Is the outcome of good anything but good?'* (Sūra al-Raḥmān 55:60), *'Have you looked at the camel to see how it's been created?'* (Sūra al-Ghāshiya 88:17) *'Do you think you will be left unaccountable?'* (Sūra al-Qiyāma 75:36). He also teaches us about constructive questions and useless questions, by narrating to us stories of people in the past who had their own questions for Him and His response to them, so that we are able to draw lessons for ourselves.

He details the story of the Bani Isra'il, who were notorious for questioning all of God's commandments, constantly asking Prophet Musa (pbuh) to make concessions for them, demanding one food over another, requesting individual paths and watering holes for each of their twelve tribes, and pushing the boundaries in looking for loopholes at every opportunity. The classic example is the story of the yellow cow (Sūra al-Baqara 2:67-73), where they are told to slaughter a cow – any cow – and strike its hide on a murdered man, who would then miraculously tell them who his killer was. They sent Prophet Musa back and forth to the mountain to ask Allah what type of cow, what colour of cow, what age it should be, etc. In their bid to evade the simple task that they had been asked to do, they only convoluted it through their useless questions, making it more difficult for themselves. In the end, they very reluctantly had to slaughter a rare and expensive breed of middle-aged, pristine, bright yellow cow, when a regular old brown cow would have sufficed!

Allah also gives the example of Prophet Ibrahim (pbuh)'s asking Him to show him how He gave life to the dead; not because he didn't believe, but for greater conviction. And Allah responds and demonstrates to him through the complete and instantaneous resurrection of four birds. Similarly, Prophet Musa (pbuh) audaciously asked to see Allah! Again, not out of disbelief but pure adoration of His beloved. Allah lovingly responded in His own way, by manifesting some of His Glory towards a mountain, but neither the mountain which crumbled nor Prophet Musa (pbuh), who fainted, had the capacity to bear His response.

Prophet Nuh (pbuh)'s question is the one that most strikes a chord in my heart and makes it quiver. I can picture him as the sky rains down vengefully, and the water level rises fast, crying out to Allah sincerely in his desperation when his own son refuses to board the Ark with him: 'My Lord! Surely my son is of my family, and Your promise is surely true, and You are the fairest of all judges!' (Sūra Hūd 11:45), Allah's response comes: 'O Nuh! Surely he is not of your family; he is the doer of other than good deeds, so do not ask Me that of which you have no knowledge; I am only admonishing you lest you be of the ignorant!' (Sūra Hūd 11:46). I cannot imagine how he must have felt in that moment: to have to trust in God's response that his own son was not to be saved, and was going to drown. And trust in God is precisely what he does; instead of protesting or pleading, Prophet Nuh (pbuh) calls out again in humble submission: 'My Lord! I seek refuge from asking You that of which I have no knowledge; and if You will not forgive me and have mercy on me, I will surely be of the losers.' (Sūra Hūd 11:47).

These stories are designed to make us introspect: Do my questions come from a place of evasion of duties and seeking loopholes, of impatiently wanting all the answers right now, or from a place of greater conviction? Do I really believe His promise that He answers whoever calls out to Him? Am I willing to patiently listen out for His responses and accept them - in whatever form they take - and will I have the capacity to bear them, if they aren't what I expect? Do I have the courage to say, 'Let me not ask what I have no knowledge of' like Prophet Nuh (pbuh), and to add: 'Only if it's good for me' at the end of all my questions, pleas and petitions?

رَبِّ إِنِّي أَعُوذُ بِكَ أَنْ أَسْأَلَكَ مَا لَيْسَ لِي بِهِ عِلْمٌ وَإِلَّا تَغْفِرْ لِي وَتَرْحَمْنِي أَكُن مِّنَ الْخَاسِرِينَ.

My Lord! I seek Your protection lest I should ask You something of which I have no knowledge. If You do not forgive me and have mercy upon me I shall be among the losers.

(Sūra Hūd 11:47 – Prophet Nuh (pbuh)'s supplication seeking refuge from asking questions in ignorance)

- Write down some of the funny or challenging questions that your children have asked you

- Have you ever struggled to answer their questions? What strategies do you use to help them discover the answers?

- What are some of the questions that you find yourself asking God, and what kind of place do they come from?

46. WEATHERING THE STORM

يَا بُنَيَّ أَقِمِ الصَّلَاةَ وَأْمُرْ بِالْمَعْرُوفِ وَانْهَ عَنِ الْمُنكَرِ وَاصْبِرْ عَلَىٰ مَا أَصَابَكَ ۖ إِنَّ ذَٰلِكَ مِنْ عَزْمِ الْأُمُورِ.

O my son! Maintain the prayer and bid what is right and forbid what is wrong, and be patient through whatever may befall you. Verily, these are matters of high resolve (courage).

(Sūra Luqman 31:17 – Luqman's advice to his son)

One of my greatest fears as a young mother was that I would fail my kids, and botch up parenting. There are many times when I have second-guessed myself, and wondered whether my decisions were to their benefit or to their detriment in allowing or disallowing certain things, in shielding them from what I thought might hurt them, or in exposing them to too much or too little. Sometimes it seemed I would never get it right, as there was always some theory or other out there about how our actions as parents could mess our kids up for life. And when I went through a completely unforeseen divorce after 15 years of marriage, my first thought was exactly that - that I had messed up parenting, and was going to fail them. My family was 'broken' beyond my control, and there was no way I could save it. My little ones were hurting and I could not protect them from that hurt. Every day I would look at them and think, *"I had one job. It was to protect them from pain, and I couldn't even do that."* When I voiced this to a wise counsellor helping me at the time, she said to me, "Give me three words to describe the kind of adults you would like your children to grow up to be?" I replied, "Kind, patient and resilient." She asked me, "So what does a human being have to confront in life to grow those kind of characteristics?" I fell silent. I knew deep down.

She continued, "Imagine your family is on an aeroplane going through a patch of turbulence. The kids are afraid. What do we do in such a situation? We look at the flight attendants. If the flight attendants lose it, we panic too. But if they seem calm, we stay calm. The parents are the flight attendants in your family, and they have been through enough turbulence in their lives to know that you will all make it. Your children are new to flying, so they're going to look to you to see whether they're okay, and whilst you can't protect them from the turbulence or make it go away, your job right now is to stay calm, reassure them, and keep serving the snacks!"

Turbulence. Pain. Storms. Challenges. It hit me then: Was it possible that I was trying too hard to protect my children from the very things that would allow them to become the people I dreamt they would be? And was it also possible that as a parent I felt like a failure because I had been assuming the wrong role? What if it was not my job - or my right - to protect my children from every incoming bump, bruise and heartache? That was it! I had assigned myself the wrong job description as a parent! It had never been to *protect them from pain* but to teach them to overcome the many hurts and difficulties that they would face in life through my own example. Maybe I wasn't botching up my job as a parent after all, and maybe this was a golden opportunity to teach them how to weather the storm outside with courage.

Life is not safe, and so our task is not to promise our kids that there will be no turbulence. It's to assure them that when the turbulence comes, we will all hold hands and get through it together. We do not promise them a heartache-free life, but we do assure them that the storms and arrows won't kill them - in fact, they will make them kinder, patient, and more resilient. We can look them right in the eye, point them to their pain, and say: "Don't be afraid, baby. That challenge was made for you. It might hurt, but it will also nurture wisdom, courage, and character. I can see what you're going through, and it's big. But I can also see your strength and courage, and that's

{ 205 }

even bigger. And we have Allah to look after us, and He's the Biggest of them all. This won't be easy, but altogether we can do hard things."

We do them no favours when we shield them from everything. Yes, of course there is a marked difference between burdening them with our adult anxieties, and between letting them experience age-appropriate hurts in the real world without jumping in to shield them: the disappointments of not getting everything they want, not coming first in every competition and race, falling and hurting themselves, failures, missed TV shows with no catch-up, broken friendships, unfair calls by the referee on the football pitch, and even bigger things like bereavement, divorce and loss.

I came across a study conducted by a developmental psychologist called Norman Garmezy in the University of Minnesota, who researched resilience in children and adults for four decades. According to him, children who grew up with a positive perception of their struggles became resilient, and those that perceived traumatic events as traumatising, flopped and slumped. Another clinical psychologist, George Bonnano, who heads the Loss and Trauma Lab in the University of Columbia, also concluded that it all lies in our perception of events: events are not traumatic until we experience and label them as traumatizing.

I knew I had to step up as their flight attendant and change their perception (and my own) of the turbulence we were currently experiencing from traumatising to strengthening, just like Lady Zaynab (pbuh) had. The grievous martyrdoms and harrowing scenes that she had witnessed in Karbala were enough to scar anyone with PTSD for many lifetimes, but she changed her perception of them from back-breaking to character-building when she famously exclaimed, *"I saw nothing by beauty"* in response to Yazid's taunts and goading.

As parents, there is no doubt that God has tasked us with the quintessential job of protecting our children – not necessarily from all pain and turbulence in this world, but - from any kind of wrongdoing that would hurt their souls, land them in real trouble, and result in pain for them in the Hereafter; *"O you who believe! Protect yourselves and your families from a Fire whose fuel will be people and stones..."* (Sūra al-Taḥrīm 66:6). When it comes to steering them away from real dangers like wrongdoing and injustice, we need to step up and be their pilots.

رَبَّنَا أَفْرِغْ عَلَيْنَا صَبْرًا وَّ ثَبِّتْ أَقْدَامَنَا وَانْصُرْنَا عَلَى الْقَوْمِ الْكَافِرِيْنَ.

Our Lord, pour down upon us patience, and make our steps firm and assist us against the unbelieving people.

(Sūra al-Baqara 2:250 – Supplication recommended when facing seemingly insurmountable challenges)

- ✥ **What are some of the painful situations that you have been trying to shield your children from?**

- ✥ **What could you do differently?**

- ✥ **What are your go-to du'as when you are facing storms and turbulence in your life? Pen them down here for your children.**

47. CALL OUT TO ME

وَإِذَا سَأَلَكَ عِبَادِي عَنِّي فَإِنِّي قَرِيبٌ ۖ أُجِيبُ دَعْوَةَ الدَّاعِ إِذَا دَعَانِ ۖ فَلْيَسْتَجِيبُوا لِي وَلْيُؤْمِنُوا بِي لَعَلَّهُمْ يَرْشُدُونَ.

And when My servants ask you about Me, then surely I am very near;
I answer the call of the caller whenever he calls on Me,
so they should answer My call and believe in Me
that they may walk in the right way.

(Sūra al-Baqara 2:186)

When my son was a pre-schooler, we lived in a house with a long garden that backed onto train tracks, and he loved to stand by the patio doors, staring outside and watching the trains go past. One fine day, a friend of mine brought her son over for a playdate, and he too was crazy about trains. As soon as she saw the glee on her son's face after having watched a train fly past, she gently got him to raise his hands up to the sky and say: "O Allah, You are so strong. Please send another train." Then she told him he had to patiently wait, and Allah would send a train. And sure enough, after a little fidgeting and waiting, to his utter delight, a train came along. He jumped up and down happily, and she coaxed him to now raise his hands and say: "Thank you, Allah". He gladly did so, then piped up, 'Again, again du'a for train.' So she helped him ask Allah for a train again, then wait patiently. And of course, as per the regular Metropolitan Line timetable (thank God!), another train rolled past, and again he joyfully thanked Allah. As this happened a few more times, he caught on quickly, asking confidently, then waiting and thanking Allah all by himself. I watched in amazement at how my friend had managed to instil the concept of *du'a*, faith in Allah's power, patience, and gratitude in her little three-year old so tenderly and beautifully, simply through an action as mundane and ordinary as waiting for trains.

That scene remained in my mind, and I excitedly related the cool teaching idea to another friend later on that week, who quizzically asked, playing devil's advocate: 'But by teaching children like that, aren't we just setting them up for disappointment in real life when they realise that God is not going to answer their every prayer, and that His responses are not as regular as trains?' True, His responses may not come as fast as trains, and they may well face delays like our trains here in London, due to various reasons that Allah knows best, but they *do* come, for He has promised to respond. And that's what we want to etch into our children's minds from young: that Allah's promise is true.

If we teach our children to call on Allah when they are little, they may just carry that habit with them for life. As they get older, our children will realise that life is full of uncertainty and heartache; that they may not get exactly what they ask for when they ask for it, or whatever they think is good for them, but they will also learn that regardless of age, we are ultimately powerless. And isn't that what prayer is all about? To surrender to our Strong and Kind God in all our neediness and poverty, because we know that in His abundance, He has all that we need. They will learn to wait patiently for the response. They will learn that the more they thank Him, the more He grants them. They will go through life with hope and confidence that there is a power much greater than them that they have access to at any time, for anything. They will remember that when they were young, Allah listened to their *du'a*, and He is always listening and responding. And what better way to teach our children the above verse where God promises to answer the 'caller whenever he calls Him'. Not the Muslim, not the believer, not the good-doer, not the fluent reciter of Arabic, but the *caller*. *Whenever* he calls.

Call out to Him today, my friend, and teach your children to call out to Him, through the fulfilment of things that they anticipate and love. Pray with them at bedtime, after *salat*, before dinner or on the way to school. Ask them what they would like to ask Allah for, and follow their lead, however silly and naïve their requests may be. Help them to articulate them. Let them hear you ask him for every little thing you need. '*Ask him for the salt in your bread, and the lace of your sandal*', as Prophet Musa (pbuh) was told to do. Ask him for the big things like faith, love and conviction. Ask him for protection and good health. Ask him fervently just like my friend's little boy asked for his trains, wait patiently for the response, then remember to thank Him joyfully. He is Powerful and Generous beyond measure. There's a reason He calls Himself *al-Mujīb* (The Responsive One).

Let them also hear you pray for others. Let them hear you pray for all the little children out there, including their friends, and their mammas. Let them hear you pray for the refugees, the homeless, the poor, the sick, the vulnerable and orphaned. Let them hear you pray for your neighbours, like Lady Fatima (pbuh) used to do so selflessly in the middle of the night. When asked by her young son, Imam al-Hasan (pbuh), why she spent so much time praying for others first, she replied, '*My son, neighbours first, then the household*.' Teaching our children to supplicate is showing them how to do life with God instead of doing it alone.

يَا مَنْ أَرْجُوهُ لِكُلِّ خَيْرٍ وَآمَنُ سَخَطَهُ عِنْدَ كُلِّ شَرٍّ، يَا مَنْ يُعْطِي الكَثِيرَ بِالقَلِيلِ، يَا مَنْ يُعْطِي مَنْ سَأَلَهُ، يَا مَنْ يُعْطِي مَنْ لَمْ يَسْأَلْهُ وَمَنْ لَمْ يَعْرِفْهُ تَحَنُّنا مِنْهُ وَرَحْمَةً ؛ أَعْطِنِي بِمَسْأَلَتِي إِيَّاكَ جَمِيعَ خَيْرِ الدُّنْيا وَجَمِيعَ خَيْرِ الآخِرةِ، وَاصْرِفْ عَنِّي بِمَسْأَلَتِي إِيَّاكَ جَمِيعَ شَرِّ الدُّنْيا وَشَرِّ الآخِرةِ فَإِنَّهُ غَيْرُ مَنْقُوصٍ ما أَعْطَيْتَ وَزِدْنِي مِنْ فَضْلِكَ يا كَرِيمُ .

O He from whom I can hope for all goodness, and I am safe from His anger at every evil. O He who gives a lot in exchange of a little. O He who gives to one who asks Him,as well as to the one who does not ask Him and does not even know Him,out of His affection and mercy. Give me - for my request is to You alone - all the good of this world and all the good of the Hereafter.
And keep away from me - for my request is only to You alone - all the evil of this world and the evil of the Hereafter.
For indeed it would not diminish what is given by You. And increase (for) me from Your bounty, O Generous One.

(Supplication recommended to be recited daily in the month of Rajab for fulfilment of all one's needs)

⸬ **Can you recall a significant time when you have called out to Allah and the response has pleasantly surprised you?**

⸬ **Do you ever have difficulty trusting that Allah's response will definitely come? Why do you think that is?**

⸬ **Can you think of a way that you can practically incorporate** *du'a* **into yours and your children's daily routine?**

48. A COMMUNITY OF MIRROR-MUMS

وَالْعَصْرِ ﴿١﴾ إِنَّ الْإِنسَانَ لَفِي خُسْرٍ ﴿٢﴾ إِلَّا الَّذِينَ آمَنُوا وَعَمِلُوا
الصَّالِحَاتِ وَتَوَاصَوْا بِالْحَقِّ وَتَوَاصَوْا بِالصَّبْرِ ﴿٣﴾

*(I swear) By Time! Man is indeed in loss; except those who believe and
do good deeds, and encourage one another to follow the truth, and
encourage one another to persevere.*

(Sūra al-ʿAṣr 103:1-3)

I have just come back from a long-overdue meetup with a beautiful
bunch of like-minded mums. We come from different backgrounds,
different family situations, and our children are of different ages
ranging from new-borns to teens, but we are all committed to our faith
and to parenting our babes as best as we can. As much as I love these
mums, we don't get together half as often as we'd like to, usually only
when there are a few overdue birthday celebrations incumbent. It is
only after sitting together with them, eating (of course!), talking and
listening, with permission to laugh at ourselves and our cringeworthy
parenting fails, celebrating our successes, and feeling thoroughly
reenergised, that I realise how much I needed it. I always come away
wishing we had done it sooner, and consider myself so blessed to have
this little community of like-minded mums in my life.

As we have become a more connected culture, mainly through
social media, we are often more disconnected from face-to-face
community, especially if we don't live close to Islamic centres.
Sometimes even when we do, we can feel lost in a large community,
longing instead for close bonds around common interests and goals.
It's very easy to become isolated with young children in the house

if wider community programs are scheduled past their bedtimes. School, sports, extra-curricular activities, work, endless housework, nursing babies, and taking care of ageing parents are all reasons that mums cut out meaningful relationships with others. Just sheer exhaustion makes community seem like a luxury for many people.

But community is not a luxury, it is a necessity. We mums need other mums to help us keep pressing on. Though it may not seem like a big deal, disconnecting from others can have a huge impact on our emotional well-being, spiritual life, and role as a mum. Doing life with others brings incredible joy. However, community also doesn't happen accidentally. Creating a community of like-minded people with similar goals, takes time and effort. And in my own life, I have found that it takes someone who is willing to step forward and initiate, be it to offer a venue, or set a date, or even just to make the suggestion; and I have always been so grateful to my friends who do so. Admittedly, I'm one of the lazy ones! But I know that if we sit back and wait for someone else to create community for us, it rarely happens. Life, and motherhood in particular, is too difficult to do alone. And it's too easy to grow weary, discouraged, or complacent in our individual Islamic practices and in motherhood. We need others around us who are also pursuing the same goals in their parenting. We need the words of wisdom, accountability, correction, and encouragement that come with being in close relationships with others.

One of my favourite sayings of the Prophet (pbuh) is: *'The believer is a mirror for a fellow believer'*, and I have always felt that it is so apt a simile for the ideal relationship between believing mums. A mirror does not lie. It reflects what's apparent, but not what you have chosen to hide, so it does not dig. A mirror does not exaggerate or distort the truth, and nor does it flatter you. It does not have a memory to keep track of past flaws. It only reflects your blemishes to you, and not to others who come to it after you. It does not make a judgment, but states facts. A mirror reflects the truth, even when it is broken. A mirror leaves you to do your own makeup and fixing: it does not step in and do it for you. A mirror has to be clean to reflect and do its job properly, so a good mirror mum-friend is one who is also committed to self-purification.

Do you have a mirror-type relationship with any mum-friends right now? Do you have other mums who have the permission to love you, listen to you without judgment, hold you accountable, and even speak the truth when you need to hear it? We all need friends like that. They are God's gifts to us, and in Sūra al-'Aṣr, when He swears by time and outlines to us how not to be a loser, He says: 'except those who believe and do good deeds, and encourage one another to follow the truth, and encourage one another to persevere.' According to Him, cooperation and motivation between believers are keys to not being losers! Don't wait for others to invite you over, or for the perfect friend to come to you; start by being one to another mum today. Reach out and take the first step. Pick up the phone. Send an email. Invite someone over for coffee. You, and others like you out there, will be so glad you did!

واجْعَلْنِي اللَّهُمَّ ... أَسْتَعْمِلْ حُسْنَ الظّنّ فِي كَافّتِهِمْ، وَأَتَوَلَّى بِالْبِرّ عَامَّتَهُمْ، وَأَغُضُّ بَصَرِي عَنْهُمْ عِفّةً، وَأَلِينُ جَانِبِي لَهُمْ تَوَاضُعاً، وَأَرِقُّ عَلَى أَهْلِ الْبَلاءِ مِنْهُمْ رَحْمَةً، وَأَسِرُّ لَهُمْ بِالْغَيْبِ مَوَدَّةً، وَأُحِبُّ بَقَاءَ النِّعْمَةِ عِنْدَهُمْ نُصْحاً، وَأُوجِبُ لَهُمْ مَا أُوجِبُ لِحَامَّتِي، وَأَرْعَى لَهُمْ مَا أَرْعَى لِخَاصَّتِي.

Let me, O God ...have a good opinion of every one of them,
attend to all of them with devotion,
lower my eyes before them in continence,
make me incline towards them in humility,
be tender towards the afflicted among them in mercy,

make them happy in their absence through affection,
love that they continue to receive favour through goodwill,
grant them what I grant my next of kin,
and observe for them what I observe for my special friends!

(Extract from Imam Zayn al-Abidin (pbuh)'s Supplication for His Friends
and Neighbours, no. 26 in Sahifa al-Sajjadiyya)

>)‏>⟨ **How can you begin to take the first step towards creating
a meaningful community of sisters around you, if you do
not already have one?**

>)‏>⟨ **How has friendship with others helped you in your
parenting journey and in your journey towards God as a
believer?**

49. SPRING-CLEANING HEARTS

إِنَّ اللَّـهَ يُحِبُّ التَّوَّابِينَ وَيُحِبُّ الْمُتَطَهِّرِينَ

Indeed Allah loves the penitent and He loves those who keep clean.

(Sūra al-Baqara 2:222)

My family and I recently started watching a new Netflix series called Tidying Up With Marie Kondo, the founder of the Konmarie Method. The series follows this Japanese spring-cleaning guru, or queen of decluttering as she has come to be known, as she is invited into people's homes to help them get rid of years of accumulated junk that no longer 'sparks joy' for them. I started watching it in the hope that it would motivate me to spring-clean my house and get rid of my junk. Ironically, it had the opposite effect as watching other people's junk made me feel a lot better about my own stuff, which thankfully was paltry in comparison to what they had amassed over the years.

In any case, it had to be done! You would think that after so many house moves, even across continents, we would have learned to accumulate less junk. But year after year, as careful as we are not to keep too many 'things', we still need to spring clean our home at least once a year. Usually in the Easter or summer holidays, we set about getting rid of 'stuff' that has accumulated in corners, on bookshelves, and in drawers. Old batteries, phone chargers, leaflets and take-away menus, unused gifts, contents of party bags, broken colour pencils, piles of paper, and dried-up markers are but a few obvious ones that come to mind. Then there are the clothes and shoes that we have outgrown or no longer wear: the faded jeans that are 'not me' anymore and the many pairs of trousers that my children seem to wear only a handful of times before they outgrow them. Old tin-openers and blunt knives in the kitchen that have outlived their purpose need throwing out too. During the process, we usually also manage to unearth beloved treasures, long lost under the sofa, behind the bed or at the back of a drawer, which is lovely and always does spark renewed joy in our hearts.

Our homes are not the only things in need of a regular, good spring-clean. At times, our hearts can also become magnets for clutter and junk. Imam Sadiq (pbuh) said, *'The believer's heart is God's sanctuary, so do not let anything else settle in God's sanctuary.'* We have to spring-clean our hearts regularly by introspecting and asking ourselves honestly: am I harbouring anger, bitterness, envy or ill-will? Have I accumulated spiritual laziness or a love that is greater than my love for God? Of course none of us intend for our hearts to become messy, or harbour dusty attitudes and contaminated thoughts, but believers have to be intentional about keeping these at bay, because unfettered clutter in the hearts can lead to sins that we never set out to commit. Allah regularly warns us about sinister things gathering on our hearts: rancour, rust, locks, sickness, veils and hardness. Hidden anger towards someone can become harshly hurled words; secret envy morphs into gossip; behind-the-scenes bitterness begets openly bad behaviour; self-deprecating thoughts cripple us from being proactive; and unchecked desires develop into damaging deeds that can destroy families. Imam Sadiq (pbuh) succinctly said, *'Hearts gather rust like the rust of copper, so polish them with repentance.'* (*'Uddat al-Dāʿī*, p.249)

Allah gives us opportunities in the form of the Day of Arafa, Laylatul Qadr, and other monumental days in the calendar, when purging our hearts through repentance is especially recommended and effective. Although seeking forgiveness is recommended daily, or weekly on Thursday nights for example, He especially facilitates for us to make an annual or regular habit of this by rewarding us for simply undertaking the process on these special days. He invites us to look deep inside the corners of our hearts, and dust them clean of any thoughts, habits, or feelings that are making us dingy and dull, and extinguishing our spark of joy. He encourages us to call on Him through His many qualities and Names that He uses to describe His actions of forgiveness. Call Him by *al-Tawwāb*: the One who turns to us relentingly, *al-'Afuww*: the One who wipes the slate clean without any trace left on it, whereby even the angels forget what they recorded, so we can stop shaming ourselves and move on. He calls Himself *al-Ghaffār* for His quality of forgiving our offences repeatedly, time and again; and *al-Ghafūr* because his forgiveness extends to all manner of misdeeds, tiny and enormous ones. He is *al-Sattār* because He conceals our shameful deeds from others' prying eyes just as we hide our junk in our closets. He is *al-Muṭahhir*, as He cleanses and polishes our hearts anew after removal of the junk.

A very effective tip that a wise teacher of mine had given us for seeking forgiveness on Laylatul Qadr, when reciting the seventy-times recommended *dhikr* of al-'Afw (literally: Sorry!) was to pencil down as many unwanted thoughts, attitudes, habits and sins that had accumulated over the past year as possible. For little ones, she suggested they simply think of a few bad things they wanted to stop doing, and put a cross on a piece of paper in pencil to represent each one. Then to go about physically erasing those markings with a brand new eraser whilst reciting sincerely: *al-'Afw*, to really make the process intentional and meaningful.

When we make the effort to humbly bring our hearts to God, admitting our shortcomings to Him alone, and sincerely asking Him to do what only He can do, He promises to forgive our sins and polish our hearts to make them new again. And it is only when we make the concerted effort to rid our hearts of the junk, that we can also unearth some long-lost cherished treasures in the process: love, joy, peace, patience, kindness, goodness, faith, gentleness and self-control.

أَللَّهُمَّ إِنِّي أَتُوبُ إِلَيْكَ فِي مَقَامِي هَذَا مِنْ كَبَائِرِ ذُنُوبِي وَصَغَائِرِهَا

وَبَوَاطِنِ سَيِّئَاتِي وَظَوَاهِرِهَا، وَسَوَالِفِ زَلَّاتِي وَحَوَادِثِهَا،

تَوْبَةَ مَنْ لا يُحَدِّثُ نَفْسَهُ بِمَعْصِيَةٍ وَلاَ يُضْمِرُ أَنْ يَعُودَ فِي خَطِيئَةٍ،

وَقَدْ قُلْتَ يَا إِلهِي فِي مُحْكَمِ كِتَابِكَ إِنَّكَ تَقْبَلُ التَّوْبَةَ عَنْ عِبَادِكَ،

وَتَعْفُو عَنِ السَّيِّئَاتِ، وَتُحِبُّ التَّوَّابِينَ،

فَاقْبَلْ تَوْبَتِي كَمَا وَعَدْتَ وَأَعْفُ عَنْ سَيِّئَاتِي كَمَا ضَمِنْتَ،

وَأَوْجِبْ لِي مَحَبَّتَكَ كَمَا شَرَطْتَ...

My God, I repent to You in this state of mine from my sins, great
and small, and all my evil deeds, inward and outward,
all my lapses, past and recent,
with the repentance of one who does not
tell himself that he might disobey
or secretly think that he might return to an offense.
You have said, my God, in the firm text of Your Book,
that You accept repentance from Your servants, erase evil deeds, and
love the repenters.
So accept my repentance as You have promised,
pardon my evil deeds as You have guaranteed,
and make Your love incumbent toward me as You have stipulated!

(Extract from Imam Zayn al-Abidin (pbuh)'s Du'a al-Tawba –
The Supplication of Repentance, no. 31 from Sahifa al-Sajjadiyya)

- What unhealthy emotion are you harbouring in your heart today?

- Spend a few moments talking to God to bring about a change of heart.

- Ask Him to bring to your mind things for which you have not forgiven yourself. Write these down in pencil, then erase what you wrote, to mirror God's ability to erase our sins.

50. TRUST, TEST OR TROPHY?

يَا أَيُّهَا الَّذِينَ آمَنُوا لَا تَخُونُوا اللَّهَ وَالرَّسُولَ وَتَخُونُوا أَمَانَاتِكُمْ وَأَنْتُمْ تَعْلَمُونَ ﴿٢٧﴾ وَاعْلَمُوا أَنَّمَا أَمْوَالُكُمْ وَأَوْلَادُكُمْ فِتْنَةٌ وَأَنَّ اللَّهَ عِندَهُ أَجْرٌ عَظِيمٌ.

O you who believe! Do not betray Allah and the Messenger, and do not betray your trusts knowingly. And know that your possessions and children are only a test, and that Allah - with Him is a great reward.

(Sūra al-Anfāl 8:27-28)

Whilst shopping for cute Islamic-themed, novelty baby vests online for my little nephew, I came across some rather interesting and funny ones like: و so cute!; I know I'm cute, don't make a س; I am God's Gift to My Parents; Sent from Above; and Bundle of Baraka. There was even one with a masked superhero baby on it, saying: Blessing in Disguise. In the end, I settled for a funny one that said, 'Oops, I just broke my wudoo again!'

It is normal and natural for parents to refer to their children as gifts and blessings from Allah, and they certainly are, as the Prophetic supplications asking for children, and Allah's granting of children all use the verb (*wahaba*), which essentially means: to gift, grant or bestow something. Children are one of the greatest divine blessings that humans can experience on earth. Unfortunately, what we often fail to realise or forget is that this bundle of *baraka* also comes with warnings and terms of usage in the Qur'an, as any good-quality gift would.

Firstly, children are referred to as **trusts** in our care, that we will be answerable for. Whilst we house and feed their bodies, and nurture their spirits - ultimately, they are not ours, but belong to God, as do we. We are but facilitators for their growth and development towards Him in this world. We are keepers of those trusts for a short time on their earthly journey, and whilst we are answerable for what we did with those trusts and how we treated them, we are first answerable for our own souls. Did I use my bounties to gain proximity to Him or did those same bounties take me away from Him? Have I lost my soul in my frenzied activity and busy-ness 'for the sake of the kids' or have my children become a means to increase my spiritual awareness? We want to protect these trusts with our lives, but ultimately it is Allah who loves them and protects them even more than we ever can. Whilst we love to do everything for them, and to have them to depend on us for their every need, we need to teach them the tools to live independently of us, to have a faith independent of ours, and to have their own relationship with their Maker.

Secondly, Allah refers to them in the verse above as **tests**, in the same vein as our possessions. Both wealth and children have often been referred to as means and tests. They are a source of happiness for us, and enable us to do many good things and to achieve our purpose on earth, but they are not the be-all and end-all according to Allah, just the means. He warns us from the very beginning, when the baby is still in the womb and his parents are praying to Allah for a good child. He says: 'When the load grows heavy, they both call upon Allah, their Lord: 'If you give us a good one, we shall certainly be of the grateful ones'. But when He gives them a good one, they set up associates with Him through the very thing He has given them...' (Sūra al-A'rāf 7:189-190). He warns us of becoming so obsessed with our children that the God who gave us that child no longer takes priority in our lives. The same child becomes a barrier to our spiritual development. All our energy is now besottedly focused on this child, through whom we live out our dreams and expectations, and treat as an extension of ourselves. Allah reminds us that our children do not exist to be our fulfilment, but they too are servants of God, with their own ambitions, personalities and paths. Allah is possessive over His servants, and He warns us not let our children, our parents, our spouses, our assets, our possessions, our businesses, our homes, and anything else be more beloved to us than Himself and striving towards Him.

Allah also tests believers in other ways through their children: through rebellious or wrongdoing children, as we see in the examples of some of our greatest prophets, like Prophet Adam, Prophet Ya'qub, Prophet Ayyub, and Prophet Nuh (pbut), all of whom were tested in this manner. A believing parent's worst nightmare is for their child to veer off the straight path, commit acts of wrongdoing or lose their faith. The test lies in how they handle this. There are some parents who lose their own moral compass in aiding and abetting their children, defending their wrong actions, failing to prevent them from doing ḥarām, siding with them even when they commit injustices. They would lose their own selves for the sake of their children. In the story of Prophet Musa (pbuh)'s encounter with Khiḍr, when Musa is horrified after witnessing Khiḍr killing a young, seemingly innocent boy, the latter explains to him his reason for doing so by Allah's command. He says: 'And as for the boy, his parents were believers and we feared he would impose rebellion and ingratitude on them.' (Sūra al-Kahf 18:80-81). They were at risk of becoming disobedient or ungrateful to God themselves due to their excessive love for their child, so God in His Mercy to them, took that child from them and gave them a pure and compassionate child instead.

Other believing parents with rebellious children may go to the other extreme of losing their peace of mind, blaming themselves, hanging their heads in shame and beating themselves up for their children's wrongs. Again, Allah reminds us that once they grow up, they are their own agents. It does not necessarily mean that we have failed as parents. We can parent them perfectly, and still have them go astray, like the children of the prophets. We are accountable for our own actions and intentions, and whilst we may desperately desire to, we cannot control how others behave, not even our kids. We can, however, pray for them through the many supplications at our disposal, and continue to remind them and guide them.

Just like the gifts of health and wealth, Allah may test us with loss: loss of our beloved children, loss of their health through sickness, allergies, disability, birth defects, learning difficulties, and disorders. Seeing any child suffer is enough to unsettle anybody, but when it comes to our own children, does seeing their pain push us parents over the edge to lose our faith in God, question His wisdom, or blame Him (God forbid)? Or does it bring us closer to reliance on Him?

Sometimes He may indeed give us a perfect child: an obedient and cooperative little angel who is calm, kind, and considerate; courageous and truthful. Then too, we must remember that the gift is a product of the generosity of the Giver. **Unlike a trophy**, it is not earned or deserved. A good child is a special gift from Allah, meriting special thanks and credit only to Him. Many people in the past have failed the test when they have attributed the goodness and success of their children, or the flourishing of their wealth to themselves. Whilst we enjoy our gifts and thank Allah for them, let us remember the warning on the packaging: 'This gift is a trust and a test - handle with care.'

رَبِّ أَوْزِعْنِيْ أَنْ أَشْكُرَ نِعْمَتَكَ الَّتِيْ أَنْعَمْتَ عَلَيَّ وَعَلَى وَالِدَيَّ وَأَنْ أَعْمَلَ صَالِحًا تَرْضَاهُ. وَأَصْلِحْ لِيْ فِيْ ذُرِّيَّتِيْ إِنِّيْ تُبْتُ إِلَيْكَ وَإِنِّيْ مِنَ الْمُسْلِمِيْنَ.

My Lord! Inspire me to give thanks for Your blessing with which You have blessed me and my parents, and that I may do righteous deeds which may please You, and invest my descendants with righteousness. Indeed I have turned you in penitence, and I am one of those who submit.

(Sūra al-Aḥqāf 46:15)

⫘ In what ways do you find your children are a test for you?

⫘ How will you ensure you pass that test?

⫘ Craft a special prayer of gratitude to Allah for your little bundles of *baraka* today.

ACKNOWLEDGEMENTS

عَن الإمام الرِضا (ع): مَنْ لَمْ يَشْكُرِ الْمَخْلُوْقَ لَمْ يَشْكُرِ الْخَالِقَ.

Imam Ridha (pbuh), 'Whoever has not thanked the creature has not thanked the Creator.'

First and foremost, I ask the Almighty, Generous One to accept all of our efforts; and thank Him for his guidance, for teaching us with His own words, and for opening our hearts to understand His Book and draw guidance and inspiration from it when we need it most. I thank Him for allowing me access to it, and for helping me articulate my thoughts into words, and for so much more that I simply cannot express here to fully appreciate. Without His Help, nothing is possible.

A massive thank you to my parents for absolutely everything you have given me and done for me. In every challenge that I have faced as a parent so far, armed with all the resources, parenting books, seminars, blogs and useful information at my fingertips, and still looking to you both for your guidance and prayers, I have marvelled at how you managed to raise four daughters in a strange land without any of those things, away from your own parents and family and all that was familiar to you, learning English as your fourth language, just to give us the chance at a good education in an environment where we could practice our faith freely. I thank you from the bottom of my heart for that *hijra* of yours, and for all your nurturing, counselling, and sacrifices. You parented us in the best way you knew how, and that was definitely good enough. I pray He rewards you abundantly and keeps your shade of mercy always over us and our children.

Thank you to my teachers and mentors who have educated me, guided me and shared their pearls of wisdom with me freely and generously.

Thank you to Tehseen, my friend and publisher, for planting the idea in my head to begin with, for your beautiful gift that inspired me, for believing and trusting in me, and for patiently waiting while I procrastinated on it for years.

Thank you to my children, for providing the material in this book, and for allowing me to use the anecdotes from your lives to give colour and illustration to my thoughts and musings, immortalising my memories of parenting you within these pages. I hope you use the journal spaces in this book to do the same for your children when you are parents, one day inshallah.

Thank you to my sisters for your continued support and constructive feedback, and for always encouraging me and rooting for me.

And last but not least, thank you to my husband: my co-parent, my rock, who has embraced the bumpy journey of parenting ever so graciously, right by my side.

Lightning Source UK Ltd.
Milton Keynes UK
UKHW020559231119
354009UK00007B/233/P